Praise for *I Wanted*

"Amy Fish is laugh-out-loud funny, and her words carry an important message: we need to stand up not only for ourselves but for everyone in line behind us. I found myself nodding feverishly in agreement. I wish I had read this twenty years earlier so I could have imparted more of this information to my children. It is so sensible."
— **Nancy Spielberg**, producer, Playmount Productions

"Self–improvement has never been easier or more enjoyable, engaging, amusing, and effective. Amy Fish delivers clear-cut instructions with passion and wit, teaching even the most reluctant complainers how to speak up for themselves. You'll laugh your way to a stronger, better you."
— **Lara Lillibridge**, bestselling author of *Mama, Mama, Only Mama: An Irreverent Guide for the Newly Single Parent*

"With warmth, humor, wisdom, and deep respect for others, Amy Fish gives you the strategies and courage to speak in your own voice to ask for what you want or need. This is storytelling and complaint handling at their very best."
— **Lydia Cummings**, university ombudsman

"Laugh-out-loud funny and packed with wise and practical advice on making your voice heard, this book should be on everyone's reading list."
— **Susan E. Opler**, ombudsman, City of Toronto

"Fresh, crisp, and terrifically useful advice. Especially good for those of us who've never had the nerve to send back a dish

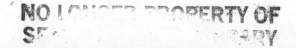

at a restaurant, these easy scripts and practical examples will help us all learn a kinder, gentler way of making things better."

— **Sam Bennett**, author of *Get It Done*

"Take it from someone who avoids complaining at all costs: Amy Fish's *I Wanted Fries with That* made me want to speak up and speak out! She offers practical advice laced with enough humor to make even the most skittish of us stand up and get exactly what we want."

— **Athena Dixon**, author of *No God in This Room*

"Amy Fish's book gave me great tips I can use at work, where I spend a lot of time negotiating with opposing counsel, and at home, where I spend a lot of time negotiating with my teenage kids. It also made me laugh along the way."

— **Susan Gradman**, Chicago attorney

Praise for *The Art of Complaining Effectively* by Amy Fish

"Amy provides a smile on every page."

— **Ruth Bader Ginsburg**, Supreme Court justice

I WANTED FRIES WITH THAT

HOW TO ASK FOR WHAT YOU WANT AND GET WHAT YOU NEED

Amy Fish

New World Library
Novato, California

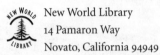
New World Library
14 Pamaron Way
Novato, California 94949

Text design by Tona Pearce Myers

Library of Congress Cataloging-in-Publication data is available.

First printing, October 2019
ISBN 978-1-60868-619-3
Ebook ISBN 978-1-60868-620-9
Printed in Canada on 100% postconsumer-waste recycled paper

New World Library is proud to be a Gold Certified Environmentally Responsible Publisher. Publisher certification awarded by Green Press Initiative.

10   9   8   7   6   5   4   3   2   1

"I ordered fries, but I'm not sure if they heard me."

— Julie Freedman, 1982

"French fries. I love them. Some people are chocolate and sweets people. I love french fries. That and caviar."

— Cameron Diaz

"A lot of people are afraid to say what they want. That's why they don't get what they want."

— Madonna

Contents

Part II: I Want You to Change

Part III: I Want Justice to Be Served

Preface

I Wanted Fries with That

You need to have the courage to live life. This includes learning to ask for what you need or want. Sometimes you are out to correct an injustice or right a wrong; other times all you're trying to do is order a side of fries.

Let me introduce you to Teenage Me. I'm with my friends. It's lunchtime. We are hungry, and we're allowed to leave school. It's Julie's turn to go to the counter and place our order. I ask her to get me fries.

There are eleven of us in a red vinyl booth that would be tight for four. I am fourteen years old and have eaten nothing but celery and egg whites for three days.* Julie returns to the table, presumably having placed our order. Fifteen minutes

---

* Huge exaggeration. Although I did follow many stupid fad diets in my day (Miracle Soup?), this is an extreme example meant to show you I was hungry.

elapse, which might not sound like a lot, but in fry time this is close to a year.

None of us have been served. I am going to pass out from hunger. My body will slide to the gummy floor and melt into the linoleum, and generations of fry eaters will tread on me until my face becomes part of the tile.

Our server arrives with pizza, subs, and a couple of salads. He is fryless.

I swallow back tears. (They are salty but lacking in crunch.)

"Jules," I say to my best friend, tucking a strand of her light-brown hair behind her ear, "what do you think happened to our fries?"

"Well, like, I went up and ordered them?" Julie speaks in questions.

"Uh-huh?" I ask.

"But, um, I'm not sure if they heard me," Julie says.

I want to SCREAM. *You're kidding*, I think. You mean to tell me that all this time, I've been waiting for french fries that we never even ordered? I've been counting the minutes, saliva gathering in my taste buds, ready to gnaw off my arm in hunger! I've been waiting for fries that were never even on their way? I want to say all this out loud, at the top of my starving lungs, but instead, I look down at the empty plate in front of me and mumble to Julie, "I wanted fries with that."

The following lessons strike me like lightning:

- Speaking up, and asking for what you need, is harder than you think.
- If you don't ask for what you want, you will not get what you need.
- If you send your friend to ask for what you want, she may

not be able to do it, in which case you won't get what you
need.

- I was born with the ability to make sure my voice is heard,
  and I need to use this gift wisely. For example, I should
  have been the one to get up and order the fries.
- Many of us need help building this skill, and it's in my best
  interest to teach you how, if only so that I could send you
  to pick up my fries next time, because Julie clearly doesn't
  have this one nailed.

Fourteen-year-old me is still in the diner. Starving.

I'd better get out of here and run to the bakery before class,
because it doesn't look like I'm having french fries anytime
soon.

Minutes later, once I have a whole-wheat bagel and a frosty
Diet Coke in my hand, and my blood sugar returns to normal,
I think about all the fries that go unordered, all the questions
that go unanswered, and all the voices that don't speak up just
because people don't know what to say or how to say it. I believe that with the right guidance, anyone can learn how to
complain effectively.

Right then and there, I commit to teach fourteen-year-old
girls ordering fries (and the rest of the general population)
how to make sure they can get what they need. How to make
sure that when any of us asks for something, we are stacking
the odds so strongly in our favor that we have the best possible
chance of getting what we want.

In other words, I commit to making sure that people know
how to complain effectively.

For the past few years, I've been Chief Complaints Officer
— also known as the ombudsman — at a huge city college
with over fifty thousand students. Students and staff come and

see me when they believe they've been treated unfairly — fries that are too soggy, fries served cold, fries that were never ordered. Just kidding. Julienned potatoes are not within my jurisdiction.

I help with exams that have been graded incorrectly, campus jobs that turned out to be not as advertised, group projects that have gone off the rails, and one memorable incident with a lab rat that — well, I've said too much already.*

Listening to complaints all day, I've amassed a giant headache. *Nah* — I love what I do. Listening to complaints all day, I've amassed a giant list of what works when you're complaining and what doesn't work, and I have a tongue-burning desire to share all this knowledge with you. In each of these chapters we will review tips for speaking up for yourself, and I will provide a real-life example for each.

---

* There wasn't really an incident with a lab rat. I'm joking.

About the Book

The Hole in the Story

The advice in this book is split into three parts. Part I, "I Want My Problem Solved," goes through typical problems that we all run into that require us to ask for a solution: how to ask for greener lettuce, how to ask the insurance adjuster to actually show up, or how to register for a 5k road race when it's sold out. Part II, "I Want You to Change," talks about asking other people to do things differently. We want them to keep the office kitchen clean or show up on time to family events. For each example, I review techniques for asking for what you want so that you can get what you need. Finally, the book finishes with Part III, "I Want Justice to Be Served." In these examples, we are looking for things to change so that the world can become a fairer place. Maybe it's too late for a personal payoff, but we want justice for everyone else — we want to ensure that no one else's grandma will trip on construction debris or that the next person will be able to ride the Pandemonium Pendulum Junior roller coaster without a shirt on.*

Each section includes seven, eight, or more stories plucked from reality, and each story illustrates a technique for standing up for yourself. So, when the 5k race is sold out, but we want a race T-shirt more than anything, we are going to be honest with the race organizer and admit where we went wrong. Then the chapter will explain the technique of admitting our own missteps and how that can help us in other situations.

At the end of each story, you get a little treat. It could be "Questions for Reflection" to help you pause and think about what you just read and how you might apply it to your own life. Or you might find an "Alternate Universe Analysis," in which we go through a similar scenario but with the facts and the outcome slightly modified.

The book is rich in colorful anecdotes, stories, and advice. Here's what it doesn't have: cold, hard science. Sure, there are a few references to studies woven throughout the text, but the core of the book is advice given by me, based on my experience as a complaint professional. I have listened to, investigated, and resolved thousands of complaints over the past decades. I have learned in my practice that some voices are heard more clearly than others not only because of the merit of their issue but also because of how they present it.

I know these techniques work for three reasons. First, I've seen them produce results — over and over and over and over. People who are calm, who speak clearly, and who — well, you'll see the rest — are better able to communicate and therefore have a better track record in getting what they want and need.

---

* Trust me, it will make sense in context.

I see people in my office every day who need help getting their message(s) across, and who, with some coaching, can step up and almost always get positive results. The majority of the time we are able to achieve these results without escalating the situation or creating formal complaints.

Second, I give talks about complaining effectively, and I usually include a Q and A where audience members line up to ask me for advice. Most of the time, people want to know how to stick up for themselves, how to be better advocates for themselves — and how I keep my skin looking so dewy. Just kidding, they actually ask about my hair. *Seriously.* Since I decided to go gray last year, my hair has become a hot topic of conversation. But getting back to the self-advocacy issue, when I answer audience questions I receive lots of head nods and applause. People often write to me and tell me how helpful my advice was. They stop me in the street to tell me that they used my advice to get their money back or their plumber to show up on time or their kids to empty the dishwasher. *Lying.* If I could get any of my kids to empty the dishwasher, I would be bottling up that tip and retiring to Corkums Island.* Point is, I receive continual positive feedback about my complaining tips and techniques, so much so that I have been flown from coast to coast to give advice about how to stand up for yourself, where again I receive positive feedback. So that's how I know it works — *you* have told *me.*

The third reason I know my tips are effective is that most of what I'm talking about is common sense, things you know deep down but don't always admit to yourself (for example,

---

* Corkums is a little island off the coast of Nova Scotia where we rented a house last summer. There is no wifi.

that people who are late will always be late). Sometimes it takes someone a bit removed from the situation to remind you that if you don't gently ask the person in front of you to unrecline her seat, you will be squished into a pretzel for the remainder of the flight.

In conclusion, the hole in the book is this: I am not backed up by double-blind subjects and external variable controls. I am backed up by decades of experience, reams of consistent positive feedback, and a good heap of common sense.

If you want your problems solved, you want other people to change, and, in general, you would like to see justice served, you've come to the right place. If you want to know about my dewy skin, my kids' reluctance to empty the dishwasher, and my decision to let my hair go gray — we can talk about that in person.

Before we get started, there's one more thing I need to tell you: I'm a chronic exaggerator. My stories are all true — basically — but I tend to add colorful details to make you laugh or think, or to protect someone's identity. Let me give you an example. In this book, I tell a story about speaking at a fancy luncheon for fancy ladies-who-lunch. That happened. I tell you that one of them asked for my advice about her husband, who is constantly on his cellphone. That also happened. But I don't remember for sure if they served crudités with salmon tartare or Pacific bluefin grilled on the roof of a car. All I can promise you is that whatever they served, it was not PB and J. I write with extensive details, even if I don't remember them 100 percent, because I want you to feel like you are at the lunch with me, admiring the silver, and wondering how they will get the lipstick stains out of the pink linen napkins.

In the world of creative nonfiction, this concept is called *truthiness*. It means that if you are fundamentally telling the truth, you can take a few liberties to tighten up your story. Acceptable liberties include these:

- Compressing time or telling things out of order
- Combining two or more characters into one to make things less complicated
- Leaving out irrelevant characters even though they were present at the time
- Adding details like smells and sounds to better describe the event or sensation
- Putting in dialogue even if you weren't recording it, so it might not be exactly what was said

Let's discuss the characters who appear in these stories. The people I am talking about exist (for the most part), but I may have given them a makeover, which could possibly include changing their name, age, and type of pet. I might make an uncle into an aunt to protect her/his/their identity or because it flows better in the story. I might make a blonde into a brunette, or a bulldog into a Boston terrier, but I will not turn a blonde into a bulldog. Unless she absolutely deserves it.

If I'm using a fake name or a fake location, or if the story is completely made up, I will warn you. For example, there's an anecdote that takes place on a treadmill. I haven't been to the gym in months, and unless there were a million bucks on the line, I'd pick the elliptical.

In every chapter, I will be giving you advice about complaining effectively that I've gleaned from years and years of dealing with complaints. The basics are there, the characters are real, the incidents all truly happened. But if I say a tablecloth was pink, and you heard it was turquoise, you might be right.

PART I

I Want My Problem Solved

Things are not going your way. You promised your daughter a Unicorn Frappuccino, but you can't find one anywhere. You have been waiting weeks for an appointment with the insurance adjuster and your emails are going unanswered. You registered late for a 5k road race, and now there are no spots left. In each of these situations, you have a problem that you want solved. And the only way to fix it is to ask.

You want to be that person. You wish you could ask for what you want and ultimately get what you need. But:

- You don't know what to say.
- You know what to say, and the words sound right in your head, but once you try to say them out loud — they get stuck in your throat.
- You're okay getting started, but if anyone says no to you, you give up immediately.
- Once you open your mouth to ask for what you want, you are so frustrated that you wind up shouting and being shrill, so no one wants to help you.

According to scientific research, consumers are known for constantly asking themselves if it's worth it to complain. We base our decision on whether we think we'll be successful, the amount of effort it takes, and the value of the product. I believe that we also base our decision on our own comfort level with speaking up: we wonder what to say and how to say it without embarrassing ourselves, causing a scene, or hurting anyone's feelings. In my opinion, many of us don't ask for what we want because we don't know how to do it gently and calmly, and still achieve the desired result.

In this first section, we will go through practical tips for how to get your problem solved, and ruffle as few feathers as possible: how to get your Unicorn Frapp, your insurance appointment prioritized, and your 5k race number in your hand, while still being nice.

How to Get Greener Lettuce

Involve the Artist

Please jump into my time machine and fasten your seat belt. I hope you haven't eaten yet, because we are headed for a submarine sandwich shop in 1996. I am on a lunch break from work.

Oh man, look how long the line is. I can't wait for my turkey sub. My favorite ingredient is the shredded lettuce. It's cold and wet and crunchy and it fills up the sub nicely. The line is moving like molasses on a snail's back. I just finished grad school, and I'm working at a hospital in downtown Toronto. Let me introduce you to my two coworkers, Ward and Ollie. We eat lunch together every day and will continue to do so for the next three years. Ward is the only person I know who actually plays the McDonald's *Monopoly* game and thinks he's going to win.* Ollie just proposed to his girlfriend, who is part Amish.

---

* My now-seventeen-year-old son, Benji, also plays *Monopoly*, believing he is about to win a free trip to Cabo San Lucas.

We are next in line. The lettuce in the display case looks a little brown. I am so disappointed. All I wanted was some nice, green iceberg.

Sandwich Artist is looking at me expectantly, twirling her lip ring with her tongue.

"Six-inch turkey on brown," I say.

"What toppings would you like with that?"

What do I do now? Do I say, "Everything except hot peppers," as I usually would, and live with the lukewarm lettuce? Or do I say, "No hot peppers, no lettuce," and eat a soggy sub that has only the half-hearted crunch of cucumber sliced paper thin?

My first reaction is to accept mediocrity. I can survive with brown lettuce. My lunch doesn't have to be fantastic. I don't have to live every moment as if it were my last. (Pinterest quotes have not been invented yet.) There will be other subs. I don't want to cause a scene.

Plus, if I do say something, she'll probably just ignore me and go on layering green peppers onto seven-grain bread with her smug latex gloves.* She doesn't care about my sub or my lettuce. There's no point in speaking up. I don't have a chance.

Oy, that is so sad. I am giving up before I even started. That's like getting to the top of the Olympic track and not rocking back and forth to launch my luge because my aerodynamic boots will probably touch the side of the ice, and I'll lose the 2.17 seconds I so badly need for the Gold. I'm not even going to try to keep my body completely still and beat my previous

---

*   I'm not sure if foodservice prep required latex gloves as early as 1996, but
     if she had been wearing them, they would have been smug.

record. I'm just going to sit here and wish I took up curling instead.

Yes, my aerodynamic boot may touch the side, and I may lose the race. But just as likely, I may win the race. I may slide down the track faster than anyone ever has, beating not only my personal best but also the competitor on my left, who I could swear illegally greased their sled. The race is fraught with uncertainty. One thing we know for sure is that I have to at least jump on my sled to get greener lettuce. Meaning, when dealing with brown lettuce, you have to try to correct it, or nothing will ever be fixed. Doing nothing is the worst possible option, and let me tell you why.

If I say nothing about the lettuce, I will have to eat something I don't want. If I get less enjoyment out of my sub, I'll have to go back to work this afternoon feeling unsatisfied. This will no doubt lead me to the vending machines, where there will be no lettuce whatsoever, and I will be forced to buy three Twix bars just to even out. I will then have to show up at my Weight Watchers meeting and announce, looking at the scale, "I tried, but the lettuce was brown." Remember, this is 1996 when Weight Watchers did not exist on your phone. People left their homes to attend meetings where they were weighed behind a supposedly opaque screen.* Alternatively, I will have the willpower to ignore the chocolate, but will spend the rest of the day feeling vaguely unsettled, like something is missing.

Another thing: If I suffer through the brown lettuce, and I say nothing, then everyone in line behind me — which at this

---

* From what I understand, these meetings still exist today, but they are far less popular than they used to be back when there were no online options.

point is like eighty-seven people — will be stuck with brown lettuce too. They will sadly pick at their steak-and-cheese, their pastrami-hold-the-jalapeño, or — even worse — their tuna salad, all thinking that if only the lettuce wasn't so brown, the sun would be shining a little more brightly today. And I will be partially to blame. I could have fixed the problem when I had a chance.

On the other hand, I can demand to see the manager. I can ask her what in the name of sliced Swiss she was thinking by putting out lettuce not just *tinged* with brown — but *riddled* with brown creeping along the edges of each and every leaf. Does she think we are fools? Not a chance! We are better than that! We are stronger! We are — still hungry because that ploy will never work.

Here's why shrieking at the manager is a no-go: It would be causing a scene. We are in a crowded restaurant, accusing the staff of doing something wrong, and embarrassing them by immediately going over their heads and speaking to the manager.

But wait, why should we be nice? They *have* done something wrong! They have attempted to serve us imperfect iceberg! They're trying to dupe us!

True, someone somewhere may have let the lettuce tray slip through quality control. But we don't know if this is a purposeful attempt to move inventory or just carelessness by people who are marking time till they can go home and soak their feet. We don't know if Sandwich Artist pointed out the brown lettuce to a manager, and she herself was told not to make waves. Until we can confirm intentional deception, I think it is in our best interest to remain calm and not raise our voices. The literature about standing up for yourself agrees with me:

"Standing up for yourself doesn't mean being a rude tyrant. There's definitely a happy medium between aggressiveness and assertiveness."

I'm worried that if we ask for the manager, we are going to stall the line. Don't forget, we have to get back to work. By the time the manager comes out, listens to our plight, and helps brainstorm a solution, hours may pass, and everyone in line will be looking at us, annoyed, and we will be embarrassed.

We've agreed that we aren't going to tolerate suboptimal lettuce. And we've agreed that asking for a manager would be premature at this point. So, what are we left with?

We can't leap over the acrylic counter ourselves and grab the fresher lettuce. That would be both unsanitary and grounds for calling 911. If we are going to get better lettuce on our subs, we need Sandwich Artist to help us. We have to get her on our side.

Watch what I do next.

Sandwich Artist has just asked me what I want on my sub. I catch her eye. I look down at the lettuce. I look back up at her, and I say:

"Does this lettuce look a little brown to you?"

She looks at the lettuce. Nods her head. Reaches below the counter, and, Hallelujah, Praise the Lord — she pulls out a fresh batch of shredded iceberg with nary a brownish leaf to be found.

What worked?

What worked is that we included the server in the conversation. We went with the fundamental belief that everyone is operating in good faith, and that all we have to do to get something corrected is to point it out. When I asked her if the lettuce looked brown, she had the chance to pause, look down at it, and form her own opinion. She agreed that it was browner than it should have been. She had the tools to correct the situation — a better lettuce supply — and she did so without any fuss.

The other thing we did well here is that we let said artist comment as an expert. Our question basically was "As someone who makes sandwiches all day long, and is very experienced in the area of lettuce, does this lettuce look brown to you?" We trusted her to give an expert opinion, and since she was empowered to do something about it, she changed the lettuce right away.

We did her a favor, because we gave her the opportunity to cast herself as the hero in the story. When we speak up, one thing we need to remember is that we are building alliances with the people who can solve our problems. This might be a sandwich artist, a clerk behind a desk, or a customer service agent on the phone. All of these people have something we want, such as new lettuce or a full refund. Sometimes all we have to do is let them see that there's a situation to be corrected and give them the chance to correct it on their own.

Now, what if she had said, "No, I don't think it looks brown" — then what would we have done? We would have pushed a little further, and maybe said something like "Really? Must be the light. From this angle, it looks kinda brown." If that didn't work, then we could maybe put a bit more pressure, with a question: "Do we have any other lettuce we can use?" Again, giving her another opportunity to save the day for us, veggie-wise.

If that didn't work either, then it would be time to evaluate how important the lettuce is, and depending on how hungry we are, how much time we have, and whether there's a line at the burger place across the street, we would make a quick decision about buying the sub now or dipping out and grabbing something somewhere else.

Before we jump back into the time machine so I can take you home, I have to congratulate you. You have learned the first lesson of speaking up.

The first lesson of speaking up is: *it works.*

Sure, it doesn't work all the time. But sometimes, it's easy. All you have to do is point out the potential problem, and the universe (or in this case, the Sandwich Artist) takes care of the rest. Had I stayed quiet, I would not have had a chance. Because I spoke up, my sub was more delicious, and I improved lunch for every single one of the 112 people in line behind me.*

The second lesson you learned today is that you can include the person you're complaining to in your complaint, and invite them to help you. Many people are thrilled to ride in on their white horses and offer you fresh lettuce.

Third, when given the chance to save the day, many people will grab it, and you will end up getting the lettuce you want and need.

When Else to Use This Technique

The "Involve the Artist" technique works well with airline or train reservations, in which case we would call it "Involve the Ticket Agent." Let's say your flight has been canceled, and you need to rebook. The ticket agent usually has the ability to fix your problem. I suggest you open by saying the lettuce looks

---

* Yeah, I said eighty-seven before, but the line is even longer now — it's lunchtime.

brown. Just kidding. That would be confusing. I suggest you open with a comment about how crowded the airport is, or a question about what time the shifts change. You can ask if the people on the flight have been losing their cool, which would indicate that you're on her side.* Then tell her that you believe in her ability to get you to your destination. Let her fingers work their magic on the keyboard, and chances are she will try to help you. If you can say things like "I'm counting on you" without being condescending, I believe it's worth a try.

Or you might want to try this technique over the phone, when you are calling to complain about something you ordered online. When the person answers the phone and says, "Hi, this is Janet," you can answer with something like "Hi, Janet. I'm so happy you answered my call. I really need your help." And then continue to involve Janet, and ask her opinion. This might sound like "Janet, I ordered the Mom Jeans in size 28, and they were too small. Are they running on the small side?" or "Have you had a lot of Mom Jean returns?" Ask questions that give Janet a chance to share some of her expertise. That will encourage her to help you. From what I understand, there is a lot of variability in what telephone customer service agents can do for you. There's no way to really ascertain what Janet's superpowers are unless you give her a chance to show you. Give her the chance.

---

* I had to pick either *her* or *him*, or the sentence would be too bulky. Don't overthink it.

How to Register for a Sold-Out Event

Admit When You're Wrong

My great-aunt and great-uncle are eighty-eight and eighty-nine years old, respectively, and I love them to pieces.* They have a summer house that they bought for about $1.50 in 1970 and has grown so tremendously in value that we probably could not afford to buy a blade of grass on that island at today's prices.† I had my first birthday there, and I have come back almost every August since. For a million years, we have timed our visit around a 5k race that my husband takes very seriously, and the rest of us try to complete in under six hours without requiring crutches, ankle tape, or a police escort.

---

* My great-auntie Dora was eighty-eight and my great-uncle Avi was eighty-nine at the time this story happened.

† I am exaggerating. I don't know the exact price or the exact date. The point is, it was way less expensive to buy vacation property in this location at that time.

Normally, my aunt and uncle register us for the race. They sign us up at the community center and then go across the street for a single slice of pizza, which they share while sitting in rocking chairs on the porch.

This year, for the first time ever, in-person sign-up is no longer an option.

All registration has to take place online, on the internet.

My great-aunt gives me this information and tells me that they are looking forward to seeing us, that they can no longer run but will be bringing lawn chairs to cheer us on, and after the race we can all go across the street for pizza, or we can do takeout and bring the pizza home.

I get off the phone with her and promptly forget everything except the promise of pizza. The place across the street from the community center makes their pies with farm-fresh toppings ranging from eggs to fennel. They have plain cheese and pepperoni too.

Several weeks pass, and it occurs to me that the sign-up for the race must be soon. I check the website, and, thankfully, I haven't yet missed the date — online sign-up is in a couple of days. I mark the date and set an alarm on my phone.

That day begins like any other. I get up, go to work, pick up my coffee at Tim Horton's on the way, and mute the alarm for online race sign-up. Check my email, mute the alarm again, do some more work, spill my XL coffee (two-milk-two-sugar), wipe up the mess, and then scroll through to see what my alarm was going on about earlier. *Oh, right — race sign-up.*

I find the website, register all five of us (my husband and me and our three kids), and click for payment. It doesn't go through.

Refresh again, use another credit card, wonder what's going on.

Race is full.

Race is full?

Race sold out in less than two hours. Registration opened at 8 a.m. and by 9:37 a.m. there were no spots to be had. It's now after two o'clock in the afternoon.

How can that be possible?

Since the beginning of time, every summer — bar none — someone from my aunt and uncle's vacation house has run in the road race. They have a commemorative T-shirt from every single year. They had a photographer take pictures of all the shirts, which they had made into a poster that they donated to the race committee. The poster was sold as a fundraiser for the race's thirty-fifth birthday.

Those T-shirts are only available to those running the race. And this year's T-shirt will now not be available to any of us, because we are not registered and therefore will not be running.

How am I going to break them the news? This is not going to be easy. I will admit that I was wrong, but I decide to put it off until I get there, hoping that once they see our brave faces, some of the sting will be gone. I will bring it up after dinner but before *Jeopardy!* That way, we'll be relaxed, but discussion will have to be quick because their show is about to start.

We drive close to eight hours, take a ferry, drive another forty-ish minutes, and pile out of the car. I bound up the stairs to greet them while Dave and the kids unpack the car. I take one look at my uncle's face, and my rational break-it-to-them-gently plan flies out the window. I blurt out immediately: "We aren't registered for the race. I tried my best but the race sold out too quickly, and I couldn't get us a spot." I am barely holding back tears. I feel so bad that this thirty-plus-year tradition is about to be broken by me, just because I muted an alarm. I didn't realize how quickly the spots would sell out.

My uncle takes both my hands in his. I kneel, so that we are face-to-face. "Amy," he says, his voice raspy. "I am really, really disappointed in you."

Oh man. Kill me now. A knife in the heart would have been less painful.

He is the last person on earth I would ever want to disappoint. And over something so preventable. How am I going to fix this? It's unfixable. I am still next to him, frozen in place, when my husband comes in and surveys the scene.

"We'll go by the community center first thing in the morning," he says. "I'm sure we'll be able to buy a T-shirt." He is completely calm.*

"No, we won't," I wail. "That's part of the shtick of this thing. You can't *buy* the shirts. You have to run the race to get them. This is a disaster."

My husband has seen actual disasters, and he knows what they look like. Missing an online registration and being short a T-shirt, even a collectible that's part of a long-standing family tradition, is not a real disaster. He tries to tell me that, but there is no reasoning with me; even Alex Trebek is not making me feel better.

The next morning, we wake up, and Dave wants to go to the community center to try our luck. I don't. He tries every persuasion technique in his husband handbook, and I am not willing to budge. "There is no way I'm going to humiliate

---

*   You know that thing where you're furious and frustrated and freaking out, and everyone around you is like still water in a glassy lake on a day with no wind, and it makes you even more tense? Yeah, that.

myself by begging complete strangers at the community center
to let me into a race that sold out fair and square," I say.

"C'mon, Amelah.* We can go across the street after, and
get pizza," he says.

"Okay fine. But I'm not going in. You can try your luck
with the race people, I'm waiting in the car."

We get to the community center, and it's buzzing with ac-
tivity. Banners and signs and balloons and music. There are
a few vendors around selling water bottles and windbreakers.
People are lining up to get their race packets and their numbers. The race is tomorrow.

Now, my husband knows something important about me
that has led us to this moment. He knows that I have no self-
control when it comes to problem solving. If you put a challenging dilemma in front of me, I will stop at nothing to help solve
it. He knows that as soon as we pull up to the race headquarters,
and we see people picking up and trying on their shirts, I will get
out of the car and try to get at least one of us (him) registered
for this race. Even though I know it's impossible. I know there's
a waiting list. I know there is absolutely no—

Wait, is that woman carrying a clipboard?

I go up to the woman. Her name tag says Donna. She
is very busy. I wait my turn. I introduce myself to her. I explain the situation, beginning with my great-aunt and -uncle
and their commitment to the race, and ending with my miscalculation regarding how quickly the registration would sell
out online. "And that's why, if at all possible, I would like to
register just one person for the race, and get them a T-shirt."

"Wait right here," Donna says. "I may be able to help you."

---

* He calls me Amelah. *Ay*-muh-lah.

She comes back ten minutes later with a registration form, a race packet, and the coveted T-shirt. She hands them to me. "I have so many people here telling me that they registered online, but the confirmation didn't go through, or that they got an email, but they forgot to print it. You can't imagine how many cats ate online registrations this year.* You are the only one that told me the truth," she says. "Thank you for being honest. You told me the truth about what went wrong, and you were genuine. That's why I wanted to help you."

Although it was painful to admit I was wrong, had I not been transparent with Donna-with-her-clipboard, she would not have been so eager to give us a registration package. What made me the most sympathetic was that I was honest and real. I explained what was really wrong, and that's why she helped me solve my problem.

When complaining, the easiest route is often the most truthful. Even though it can be hard to concede your own mistakes, it's worth it if you get to come home bearing good news, a coveted T-shirt, and of course, a broccoli rabe–spinach–pesto pizza for lunch.

Questions for Reflection

1. Is being right important to you? Can you think of a time where being right got in the way of figuring out a solution to a problem?

---

* Yes, I can imagine, because *The Cat Ate My Gymsuit* by Paula Danziger was my sister's and my favorite book growing up, and we read it so many times that we used to play fill-in-the-blank where one of us would read out loud and the other would have to remember the missing words. Maybe we should have watched more TV.

2. Would you choose the 5k or pizza? Be honest.
3. Is there anyone in your life you would hate to disappoint? Would this prevent you from speaking your mind or encourage you to speak up?

How to Get the Insurance Adjuster to Show Up

Put Yourself in Their Shoes

You need to meet my friend Melanie, interior designer to the stars. Hockey players in town for the season, CEOs moving to country estates, successful tech entrepreneurs — they all want Mel to "do" their homes. Her style is so modern it hasn't been invented yet. Because of the nature of her work and the gargantuan size of her bank account, Melanie changes homes every seven to nine months. This story opens when we drop by Mel's latest concrete box, a penthouse loft in what used to be a boat repository, or an ancient rectory, or a munitions factory.

"And this is the dishwasher," Melanie says, pointing to a drawer that, from the outside, looks nothing like a dishwasher. She discreetly pushes a button and, just like on *Luxury House Hunters*, the drawer opens, and lo and behold, there is a tiny rack, perfect for washing the one wineglass and bowl of popcorn that would be considered dinner dishes in this context.

"I love it," I say to her, noting that her open shelves are too small to store anything purchased at Costco.

"Me too," she says. "It's so much better than the one I had before, that caused all this damage." She points out the bumps in the warped wooden floor and the stain along the floorboards.

"That wasn't on purpose?" I ask, not joking. As I said, her style is so avant-garde, I heretofore assumed that warped wood was the next big thing and was on my way home to run the faucet over my dining room floors just to be in the loop. Good thing she clarified.

"Ha-ha, Amy. Very funny. Obviously, this was because of the last dishwasher," she says. "I'm so annoyed. I've been on the phone with my insurance company for weeks trying to get this fixed."

My ears perk up. I love talk of insurance companies and unresolved complaints.

"What's happening?" I ask.

"So. Annoying."

I wait, so she'll continue.

"I told the insurance company that I needed them to fix the floor so I can proceed with my renovations. That should be a priority. Especially since I'm putting this place on the market," Mel says.

"You're putting this place on the market?" I ask.

"Yes, of course. I've been here for four months. I bought an ice-fishing cabin on the lake, and I move in three weeks, which gives me just enough time to break down the inside walls and install a fireplace in the powder room."

If anyone can make an ice-fishing cabin into a five-star luxury retreat, it's my friend Mel.

Melanie shows me the email that she has sent to the insurance company asking for assistance. The subject heading reads ***URGENT***. The body of the email runs through the damage to her floors and explains that this has to be taken care of ASAP because she has in-floor lighting specialists scheduled to install miniature LED lights in the oak, and that project must be completed before she can fly the custom cabinet guy in from Antwerp to build her 1,800-square-foot shoe closet with a revolving rack for suede boots.

I've known Melanie since she was sharing a bed with her grandma and lining up for free breakfast before class. She has earned every carat on her wrist. Every soon-to-be-installed LED light in her oak flooring is a result of her hard work and determination. That's why she probably doesn't really realize how she sounds to the insurance clerk processing her claim.

Let's put ourselves in the shoes — the imitation suede booties — of the person who opens Mel's email.

Imagine that you work in a gray cubicle. You have last year's cat calendar pinned to your wall next to a few quotes that used to be motivational. You drink your coffee from a company mug that you only rinse out once a week, so it has rings of history like those of the famed redwood tree. Your inbox is packed because you were off Monday dealing with Junior's school. Again.

You sift through your ugly pile of work and come across an email labeled ***URGENT***. You are picturing fire victims huddled under pale-blue blankets. Women fleeing abusive relationships at 2 a.m. A foster home with no heat, no electricity, and no running water.

Instead, you read three paragraphs about a floor installer,

and how complicated it is to put LED lighting into oak. Melanie's floor emergency.

Are you thinking this deserves your immediate attention? Or are you more likely to help the clients who are filing insurance claims because they have nowhere to sleep tonight?

That's what I thought too.

"Melanie, I can help you," I tell her. "We can write to the insurance company and make your claim more compelling."

"Why should I have to lie?" she asks. "I don't want to invent homeless donkeys or black mold infestations just to get my flooring replaced."*

"I agree. We will not lie. I am merely suggesting that we showcase the elements of the story that are likely to gain more sympathy while perhaps playing down the pieces that are a bit more, shall we say, upscale?"

I go on to explain that, ideally, email requests will be responded to in the order in which they appear. And in my experience that's basically true, but some things will get pushed forward (or back) a little more quickly, based on interest, priority, and number of lives that need saving. A message might be more of a priority if it's called something like *Help Needed, Please* instead of ***URGENT***. Although Mel's request is urgent to her, we can't oversell the urgency when trying to get someone to hear our voice. Being realistic may move her closer to the top of the queue.

For best results, the body of the email should be as straightforward as possible and include a reason why action

---

* If you are interested in homeless donkeys, I read a great book about the problem called *Saving Simon: How a Rescue Donkey Taught Me the Meaning of Compassion*, by Jon Katz. Highly recommend.

is necessary. For Mel, I suggest an initial email like this: "I am writing to you because I need your help. There was a leak in my apartment, and my floors need to be replaced. Before I can have the work done, I need to have someone from your company come by and check it out. Please let me know how we can get this set up as soon as possible. Thanks." If Melanie wants to include some time pressure, she can mention that she is moving, and this apartment is going on the market in a couple of weeks. That is relatable. No one wants to carry two rents or mortgages, and everyone understands that moving houses is high-stress.

Mel sends the email.

A couple of days later, the insurance company sends an estimator, and by the weekend Melanie's warped floor is replaced. The twinkle lights are installed in the new oak flooring, and the gargantuan shoe rack is built.

Melanie's complaint was legit. She should not have had to wait extra long for service just because her condo is on a certain block or her dishwasher is especially sleek. Sometimes, though, it doesn't hurt to imagine the person on the other end of your complaint and see if you can appeal to them directly.

Alternate Universe Analysis

If Mel's attempt to put herself in the insurance clerk's shoes didn't work, I would have suggested that she consistently keep in touch with the office. Let's say she sends an email and doesn't get an answer. She waits two or three days and forwards the email back, saying something like "I'm not sure if you had a chance to look at my email below. As you can see, my apartment was flooded and..."

If she does not get a response to the second email, then she can attempt to reach the insurance company over the phone. She will say, "I sent an email to [person] on [date], and again on [second date]. I haven't had an answer yet. Is there someone else I can try?" or "Is there another email address I can send this to?" or "Is there any way you can help me?"

Then she writes down the name of the person she spoke to, and she follows up with an email to them, saying, "Thank you for helping me over the phone today. As I mentioned, I've been trying to get in touch with [person] from the claims department since [date]. Anything you can do to help expedite this would be very appreciated."

And she continues, until the company realizes that she is not going anywhere, and they might as well help her. She can go up the chain asking for a manager, in which case she should have in front of her all her dates and times so that she can say something like "Thank you for taking my call. You are the eleventh person I have spoken to. This has been going on for three weeks. [List people, dates, and calls.] Please let me know what we can do to take care of this problem."

By continuing to call every day or two and then sending emails, Mel will have a strong track record that she can use to follow up.

How to Get the Person in Front of You to Move Their Seat Up

Go Step-by-Step

I am on the phone with Georgia the Acquisitions Editor, and she is excited about my nonfiction book proposal. So excited, she might actually make an offer to buy the manuscript. Which ultimately she does, and I am super grateful to her and the entire team, but let's not skip ahead. We are on our first phone call, and I'm trying to impress everyone without looking like I'm trying too hard. Sweat is pouring down my brow.

To illustrate the kind of thing she would like to see answered in the book about standing up for yourself, complaining effectively, and making sure your voice is heard, the example Georgia keeps going back to is the airline seat: "What if someone reclines their seat too far back into your space?"

Here's the thing, though. I base my book on stories that actually happened, either that were told to me or that I experienced myself. But I'm too scared to tell this to Georgia because

(a) I want her to like me, (b) I want her to buy my manuscript and turn it into a book because she sounds like she knows what she's doing, and (c) the last time I was on the phone with an acquisitions guy I couldn't hear a word he was saying, he kept cutting out, and after the second or fourth "I'm sorry, I think we have a bad connection," I had to just suck it up, and to this day I have no idea what I agreed to.

Putting this together, I'm going to give you a made-up example that never happened to show you how to complain effectively if the person in front of you reclines their seat into your airspace.

Pretend that I am on my way to Toronto for an ombudsman meeting, and the flight is one hour long. I have packed enough work, knitting, and podcasts to make it to Antarctica. I will start with the work because this is an imaginary story, so why not look productive?

As soon as I'm allowed to, I undo my seat table and organize my laptop. The older woman in front of me reclines her seat all the way back so that I would have to hold my elbows next to my ears to type. I am no good at Pilates.

The first thing I do is get out of my seat so I can look the woman in the eye. It's too easy to ignore a voice floating behind you. Then I calmly give her the information: "Excuse me, your seat is reclined all the way back, and I can't do my work."

Today, this causes an immediate reaction. The person says, "Oh, I'm sorry," and puts her seat up right away. I politely say, "Thank you," and go back to my seat and do my work.

Other times, the person might say, "Well, I'm comfortable like this," or "Too bad for you," or anything else rude. In that situation, you go back to your seat. Then you press the light to call the flight attendant. When the flight attendant comes, you calmly gesture to the seat reclined all the way back and say, "I'm so happy you're here. I need your help. I need to get my work done, and this passenger has reclined their seat all the way back. I can't reach my computer like this."

The flight attendant might gently suggest to the person in front of you that they move their seat up. If this works, you thank everyone, and once again, you are left with no choice but to actually do your work, because if anyone looks over and you are not typing, you will look like an animal.

The flight attendant might also say to you, "The seats move back this far. There's nothing we can do about it."

If this happens, you say something along the lines of "I understand. My problem is that I'm working on a deadline (or a presentation, or a term paper — whatever is accurate or the closest to accurate you can be), and I can't type like this."

This may be sufficiently convincing to get the flight attendant to help you and ask the person to move up. If it doesn't work, then you go to your next level: Ask for something else. "If I can't get this person to move up, is there any other seat I can move to?"

The flight attendant may have another seat that is behind someone who is not reclined that you can move to. If they offer you this, you will gracefully put all your stuff together and follow them to the new location. Questions such as "How will I get my bag later?" would be annoying under these circumstances because you asked to be moved, and you got what you wanted. I'm going to answer for the flight attendant: If you can carry your bag, bring it with you now. If you can't, then make two trips, and if that doesn't work, get your bag when everyone deplanes.

If you are traveling with companions and you need to sit

with them the whole time, then make this clear when you ask for another seat. For example: "Do you have another set of seats *we* can move to?" Alternatively, you will have to make a choice between sitting where you can work and being next to your friend/coworker/three-year-old child.

Now, let's say the flight attendant is not willing to help. Let's say he/she is busy or having a rough day or believes that the seats recline the way they do and that it's everyone's right to go back as far as the seat allows regardless of how annoying it is for other passengers. In that case, you look around and see if there's a seat that you can move to. You can ask again, indicating a specific seat, for example: "Can I move to seat 15D?" Or you leave your stuff in your spot and walk over to 15D to make sure it's vacant, and then ask 15C or 15E if the seat is indeed vacant and if you can move there.

Another option is to look at the people immediately around you and see if any of them look like the types who would switch seats with you. That might be worth a try too. Especially if you can ask calmly.

If none of this works, you can go back to the person in front of you and ask again. Say something like "Excuse me, I know you are trying to relax, I just really need some help here. I tried to change seats, and there's nothing else available. This is a full flight. I have a deadline when we land. If you could move up a bit so that I could do my work, that would really help me." If that sounds too nervy to you, then you may have to give up for now.

In a case where you are unable to resolve the seat situation during the course of the flight, the complaint is not over. Jot down your seat number and the name of the flight attendant who was not particularly helpful. Then write a complaint email or fill out a survey indicating your lack of satisfaction with the seat-reclining angle and the way the flight attendant handled the situation. I would ask for a written response to my complaint or for someone to call me. Even though that would not resolve my problem in the short term, it may produce a solution for other travelers in the longer term — for example, maybe seats will not be built to recline so far, or maybe the plane will eventually have a nonreclining section for those of us who need to use our laptops or are unhappy with having complete strangers lolling about in our laps.

Recording your dissatisfaction is important because the airline may collect data about these kinds of problems. The next time they are sitting around a table wondering how far back seats should recline, you want someone to be able to say, "We have received a bunch of complaints about the seats moving back too far," so that someone else can say, "Oh, let's take a look at it then."

If no one ever says a word about the seats going back too far, then next time they may be designed to go back even further. The same is true of the flight attendant's attitude. If they won't help you, and you say nothing, then their file will be empty, and when it's time for a raise or a promotion or a new opportunity, there will be no reason for anyone in Human Resources to stop it. But if you speak up and send a written complaint, the next time this person has a review, a complaint will be discussed.

I want you to get a few lessons from this airline seat example. First, you start slow and gentle. Let the person know what the problem is, and give them a chance to fix it. If that works, you're on Easy Street. Second, if the first, most direct route doesn't work, try any creative alternative you can think of while remaining calm and polite. Third, if neither of those works, ask for help from an authority, in this case the flight attendant. And fourth, even if you are at an impasse and can't budge anyone in this specific situation, your responsibility as a complainant is not over until you have let the company — the airline — know what happened so that they have a record for future reference.

Wow, that was a lot of information to squeeze out of one reclining-seat example, especially since the imaginary flight was only an hour long. I guess that means there is a fifth lesson learned here. If your editor is sufficiently invested to actually purchase your book, and there's something she wants you to include, you should probably listen to her.

When Else to Use This Technique

This is a good technique for when you are trying to get someone to do something for you that they really don't have to do. For example, say you would like to renew a library book that is not really renewable. You can ask the librarian to let you renew it just this once and explain that you need the book to read it for your book club — which would not be realistic in my case because my group has a great time together but we rarely read books. Or maybe you need to read the book for a class. Explain your reason, and see if you can appeal to his compassionate side. Let me give you a few examples:

- "It says here that this book isn't renewable, but I haven't finished my report yet, and I need the book to finish. Is the due date flexible?"
- "Hi, I'm wondering how strict the renewing policy is? I have to read it for class, and I'm not done yet."

- "Is there any way I could extend my borrowing window a couple of days? I'm so close to finishing this book, I have like thirty pages left. If there was any way I could get an extension of a day or two, it would help me so much."

If none of these reasons work, you can just start asking details about the rules. Ask if there are fines for not respecting the return date. Ask how much the fines are, what happens if they aren't paid, whether you can pay online.

Just as in the airplane seat example, if the librarian can't help you, think of alternatives that will solve your problem. Instead of looking to switch seats, see if your library has an ebook program that you could benefit from or if there's an audiobook you could borrow that would not violate the rental agreement. (I would suggest watching the movie instead, but we know that's often not the same as reading the book.)

If you are absolutely unable to borrow the book or find another solution, I suggest you email the library and let them know about your dissatisfaction. You might indicate that you find the borrowing windows too short or the renewal periods too stringent.

While it can be a chore to go the extra mile and lodge your dissatisfaction officially, I believe this is the only way we can get things to change.

How to Get Your Appliance Repaired

Be Clear and Concise

My stove is moody. The burners sometimes stop working, and I have to call the stove company to come and take a look and make an adjustment.

When I am on the phone with them, it's tempting to start at the beginning, when we bought this house twelve years ago. I think it was twelve because my daughter was about one, and we moved in just before Halloween. I remember it was my goal to have Halloween in the new house. At that time, there was a functioning stove in the kitchen, but it looked like it had seen better days, so we scrapped it and bought a new model. You can imagine that the move cost us more than we thought it would, as these things usually do, so our new stove was whatever was on sale at the big box store that Sunday, without a big investigation — or any investigation of any kind, to be honest.

Now, let's say I have said all this to the customer service

representative at the other end of the phone. I have used up about half a minute, and I still haven't told her why I called. She is not interested in the age of my house, the time of year I moved, or the day of the week the stove was purchased.

"Is there anything I can help you with today?" she asks.

My best bet is to be as concise and specific as possible. "Yes, I am calling because I need someone to look at my stove. Three of the burners will not heat up at all. The model number is 875C."

I can also take this opportunity to ask questions, such as these:

- How much will it cost to send a repair person to my house?
- If he or she can't fix the stove on the spot, will I still be charged for the visit?
- Does this problem happen often, and do you have any idea whether it is usually fixable?

In this scenario, I have the model number with me, and I have planned ahead as to what I want out of this phone call. I want a service appointment, and I want more information.

Sometimes the customer service person will not be helpful. They will not have read the study of Ugandan mobile phone subscribers that suggests that the greater the service quality of the customer service representative, the more likely the customer is to be loyal in the long run. I assure you that if the customer service rep had read it, they would be way more likely to give me a hand. Companies with a lesser commitment to quality will give me an appointment for between 10 a.m. and 3 p.m. after I have said that doesn't work for me because I'm at the office in the middle of the day.

In that case, I may be tempted to say, "Oh, I'll see if I can get Stan to cover for me at 10 a.m., I helped him out when his daughter got married. But 3 p.m., that's going to be tough." This too is not Customer Service Agent's concern. He needs to know whether he can put you on the schedule for between 10 a.m. and 3 p.m., and he needs an answer.

This doesn't mean that you should just say yes, suck it up, and either get in trouble at work or take an unpaid day, depending on your circumstances. It means that now you can ask other questions to determine if there are alternative times for this appointment.

You can say, "Thank you for responding to me so quickly. Unfortunately, I'm at work during those hours. Do you have anything early morning/late evening/on the weekend?" Or, "Is there any way you can provide a narrower window? Five hours means that I have to miss a whole day of work." People usually understand that because everyone has to work, and no one wants to miss a whole day waiting for a repair person.

If you live close enough to your workplace, and if your schedule is sufficiently flexible, you may say: "Would the technician be able to call me when he gets close? That way, I can meet him at the house?" I learned that from my husband, who mercifully works for himself and has an office less than fifteen minutes away from our house and can usually be home in time to deal with repair people. It is surprising how many companies (even giant ones like the cable installers) will agree to this plan.

Let's modify the scenario slightly. Let's say that the last time this repair company came to fix something, the technician left on her boots and tracked mud all over my floors. I never complained about it at the time. I have decided to call back the same repair company because they were successful in fixing the washing machine, but I would like to mention how much that event aggravated me. I call and say, "Hi. I've called you guys before, like three years ago? Because my washing machine wasn't working, the whites weren't coming out clean? You sent a girl technician, is that politically correct to say? A technician that was female? She left her boots on, and it took weeks to get her footprints off my carpets. Anyway, I'm calling now because my stove isn't working and…"

In my mind, I feel that I have officially complained about the footprints. But the person taking my call might register this as background noise and not necessarily as an official complaint. If I would like to complain about the boots and the mud, I should have really done it at the time, or closer to the time, when I would have had all the relevant information. My call would have sounded like this: "Hi, this is Amy Fish. I'm calling about work order number 3717. The technician was here today and did not remove her boots. It is raining out, and now there is mud on my floor." If I want compensation, I could add, "The total repair invoice is for $247. How much are you willing to deduct for cleaning service?" I could also take pictures of the muddy floor and send an email to the company saying, "Dear [person's name], I am writing to follow up on the work done at my house [insert address] last Tuesday. The washing machine was fixed — thank you for that. Unfortunately, your technician did not remove her boots, and I spent $172 having my carpets cleaned. Attached please find photos of the damage to my carpets as well as a copy of the carpet-cleaning invoice. I have adjusted my payment accordingly."

Maybe at the time of the original repair, I didn't follow up as quickly as I now see I should have. Maybe my cat was favoring her left paw, and I was worried. Maybe I had just broken up with my boyfriend. Maybe I needed a pedicure, and my big toenail looked so gross that it was all I could think about. I understand that speaking up is not always a top priority. Don't despair, you can still mention the mud during this call, but I wouldn't want to distract from the main point of the conversation, which is getting a repair appointment for the stove. I would first explain what I need today, and once I have the appointment time established, then I would say something like "While I have you on the phone, a few years ago you sent someone to our house and they forgot to remove their boots. Tracked mud everywhere. Can you please make a note in the file that the technician needs to take their shoes off this time?"

Part of speaking your mind includes speaking clearly. If you give too many details or too much background or take the listener on a winding story, the person you're complaining to may not know how to help you because they may not know what you want.

Be simple and straightforward, and ask for what you want as an outcome. Storytelling is great, around a campfire or among friends. But when it comes to getting something in your house repaired, I believe your best bet is to be as clear and as concise as possible.

Questions for Reflection

1. Are you more likely to go on and on and on, or to be concise when telling a story?
2. What makes you talk for a long time? Is it that you have a lot to say or that you use extensive detail? Think about how

you could tell your stories using fewer words in the future. Where would you cut? Would the essence be missing?

3. Do you agree that there's a difference between sharing an interesting anecdote and conveying information necessary to get your point across? Think about circumstances where each is more appropriate.

How to Get Clingy Children to Back Off

Use the Resolution Continuum

It is 8 a.m. on a Sunday in August, and I am at a chain hotel in British Columbia drinking mass-produced coffee. We're at a post-wedding breakfast, sitting with distant cousins on my husband's side who have kids much younger than ours — maybe seven- or eight-year-olds. I bring up complaining as a conversation topic (I know, I know, don't ever sit next to me at a post-wedding breakfast). Specifically, I want to know how they teach their kids to stand up for themselves.

The person I know least at the table, let's call her Lindsey (we have to give her a fake name since I don't remember her actual name), says her son, fake-named Cal, is in second grade, and his biggest problem is that one of the other kids in his class wants to play with him every recess and lunch. While this sounds sort of sweet — especially for those of us whose kids benefit from "buddy benches" and conversation groups — I

can see where it could be a lot to navigate for the little guy.*
The mom, fake Lindsey, is not sure what to do about this because it's causing her son so much angst.

Lindsey is wondering if she should call the school and ask
the teacher to intervene, or if she should call the other kid's
mother and ask her to tell her son to back off a bit and give
Lindsey's son some breathing room.

I don't like either of those options.

Cousin Nadivah, also sitting at the table, wonders if maybe
fake Cal should just play with whomever he wants, and if the
other kid gets insulted, well, that's the price of being clingy.
Or, Nadivah says, maybe Cal needs to stay home from school
for a few days — heck, it's only second grade. Let the kid make
some new friends so that when Cal comes back, the coast will
hopefully be clear for him.

I guess that's a choice. Education is overrated.

Lindsey has the chance to teach her kid how to ask for his
own fries — I mean navigate this situation on his own. The
first thing he needs to figure out is what he wants to happen.

When you are trying to figure out what you want as the
outcome to a complaint, sometimes it's helpful to think in extremes. I tell Lindsey to explain to her son that there are two
main options. One is to keep things exactly as they are and play
with this kid every single day at every single break. The second
is to ditch the kid entirely, and never play with him again.

Chances are Cal won't pick either of these options. That's

---

*   Buddy benches are dedicated to kids looking for friends. Kids who want
someone to play with sit on the bench and that lets the other kids know
to invite them to play.

when Lindsey explains to him that the best solution is hiding somewhere in the middle.

I call this the *resolution continuum*. It's adapted from a methodology that I learned when I was a consultant in the early nineties. I was the lowest rung on the ladder (actually, below even the lowest rung), and I wore pantsuits every day, just so you can picture me. We provided management consulting services to the health and social services sector. When a client had a problem that looked unsolvable, we would put the problem on a continuum. On the extreme left, we had status quo: what would happen if we kept doing things exactly the same way and nothing changed. All the way on the right, we would put extreme change: what would happen if we did the exact opposite of what we were doing now. And then, moving along the middle, we would work with the client to generate possible options that would be ranked according to degree of change. This is often a helpful tool in determining what you would like as the outcome to your complaint.

Let's imagine that fake Lindsey and Cal are swinging in the park after school, reflecting on this playground situation. Lindsey explains the resolution continuum to Cal, and he agrees that the ideal solution lies somewhere in the middle.

Lindsey now says, "Let's think of ideas that could work."

If you and I were brainstorming, our list would probably look something like this:

- Cal plays with the kid at first recess and plays with other friends at lunch (or the reverse).
- Cal offers to play with the kid at all breaks on Mondays and Wednesdays if for the rest of the week he's on his own.
- Cal continues to play with the kid as long as they can include other friends in their games.

- Cal plays with whomever he wants, and the kid is always welcome to join.
- Cal agrees to having a standing afterschool playdate with the kid once a week if the kid settles down about recess obligations.

In my experience, kids are great about generating more obscure alternatives that relate to things that adults would never think of, so let's imagine Cal adds the following to the master list:

- I'll play with him if he wants to run near the big tree, but if he goes on the side playground then I want to play with Sam.
- I'll play with him if he doesn't throw the ball in the mud; he thinks it's funny, but I don't want to go back to class with mud on my sweatpants.
- I'll play with him if he goes to indoor recess; I hate playing outside.

Now Cal has a better idea of how to negotiate this interaction. He can use his own words to tell the kid things have to change because he knows what change he's looking for. He may even decide to give the kid a few options.

Cal knew that he was unhappy being trapped playing with the same kid at every recess and break every day. He also knew that he wanted to remain friends with him. So, the desired outcome is a compromise.

When you are facing a similar dilemma, go immediately to a post-wedding breakfast in British Columbia, and ask people what they think. But first try the oatmeal, it's better than it looks. Just kidding. Have a blueberry muffin, you're on holiday. But seriously, when you are facing a similar dilemma, I urge you to try this technique to figure out what you want. You can draw the continuum out on a piece of paper, like a time line, or think about it in your head. Sometimes thinking in extremes can help you figure out what you are really looking for.

Once you know what you want, then you can ask for it.

Questions for Reflection

1. In this story, Lindsey is trying to help her son come up with a solution for his problem. Are you more likely to be in the position of Lindsey or Cal? Do you call on people for advice or are you an adviser? Think about your usual role in your relationships. If you are the helper, think about what problem-solving techniques you usually rely on. Would the continuum help you? If you are the seeker, think about whether this tool could help you generate options before you ask for advice, or whether it would be an interesting discussion guide going forward.

2. So many of us are stuck in our behavior patterns. Are there any "go-tos" that you rely on in problem solving? I invite you to reflect on your typical techniques. Are you looking for new ways to think about things? Ask yourself if using a structured methodology like the continuum would help you. Think about possible situations where it might have helped you in the past, or where you might apply it going forward.

7
How to Exchange a Onesie (When You'd Rather Get Your Money Back)

Be Prepared to Compromise

I am on my way to a conference in Edmonton, Alberta. I know that they have the largest mall in North America, but since I used to live in Minneapolis near the *second* largest mall in North America, I can give this tourist attraction a pass. How much Salted Pinetree Rose Soap and Honeycrisp Apple Fine Fragrance Mist does anyone need, even if you buy two and get the third for 25 percent off?

Looking at the conference schedule, I see that there is nothing planned for the evenings, and I imagine myself sitting alone crying into my hotel pillow. But, alas, there are knitting stores in Edmonton, and knitters will keep me company. I call the one that looks the friendliest and see if they are interested in a "Stitch and (Learn to) Bitch" evening where I talk about complaining and everyone sits around and knits. Their excitement surpasses my wildest dreams. Not only do they book me for two consecutive nights, they sell tickets to the events and design a knitting pattern in my honor. And. They offer to pay in yarn. Pinch me.

I am greeted by a chalk sign announcing my arrival. *May keel over and die from happiness.* Except, oddly, they have advertised that the event is two and a half hours long, and I am the only speaker. I can be super chatty, and complaints are definitely my favorite topic of conversation, but when we pass the 120-minute mark, even Mork from Ork could be a little boring (may he rest in peace).*

After my usual blah blah, I open the floor for questions and comments, and Florence raises her hand. She is knitting a Fair Isle cardigan in pale peach with hints of ivory and mint green.

Florence is very upset about her recent shopping experience.

"Tell us what happened, Florence," I say and glance at the clock. "We want every detail."

"I was invited to a baby shower. My sister-in-law's grand-baby," she says. "They rented out the Omni Hotel and had sushi chefs flown in from Tsukiji market. They tried to get Jiro from the subway, but he fell through at the last minute."

"Yo, Flo, was there a baby registry?" asks Jojo. She is knitting a skull-and-crossbones sweater for her pit bull, Alice.

"No, and I wish there was. I went to this boutique because I needed something that, er, that, um…"

"That looked expensive. It's okay, Florence, we understand," I say.

"And I pick out a onesie—"

"What's a onesie?" Kevin asks. You'd think a male knitter

---

* Mork was a character played by Robin Williams on an old TV show.

would magically understand everything about the world of women, but there are some topics that remain estrogen-only, such as baby undershirts that snap under the diaper — aka, onesies.

Florence continues with her story. She meanders around the point, which would normally drive me up a wall, but we are on a reverse race against the clock here — we want to use up time — so I'm more patient than usual.

"I choose a darling hand-embroidered onesie with little poppies around the collar and cuffs. Ninety-three dollars. I walk out of the store and immediately realize I have spent (almost) my monthly grocery budget on one baby gift. It also occurs to me that I avoided knitting for the baby because I thought a handmade gift was gauche, only to spend a king's ransom on a handmade gift not even made by my hands!"

"So what'd'ja do?" Jojo asks.

"I walked back into the store and asked to return the poppy onesie."

"And?" I ask.

"The girl behind the cash register says, 'No refunds.' I say to her, 'That cannot be possible, my dear. I just bought the onesie. I walked out of the store and realized my mistake. And now I would like to return it,'" Florence says.

Poor Florence. I am listening to this story and feeling so irritated on her behalf.

"The girl points to the sign over her head and says to me — she says, 'Oh, I'm sorry, is the writing too small or whatever? The sign says No Refunds.'"

"You can tell she wasn't the owner. The store owner probably would've let you change your mind," says Lauren, our knitting-store proprietor and hostess for the evening.

"How do you wash the poppy onesie without the colors running?" asks someone from the back of the room.

"You soak it in cold first," Florence says. "Gran used to swear by a mixture of one part baking soda and—"

Before we can share Gran's home detergent recipes from the backwoods of Alberta in 1909, I take back the microphone.

"Florence, did you ask if you could exchange the onesie for a gift certificate? It's not nice to say, but at least then your sister-in-law would know how much you spent, and you would get full credit for it," I say.

"No way," Florence says. "If I can't get a refund then I'm not interested in no gift card."

Let us pause here for a moment. Florence has inadvertently purchased a gift that she no longer wants to give. She asks for her money back and the clerk says no, because according to strict interpretation of company policy, no refunds are available. Florence is insulted. She is stuck in the unfairness. She believes that she should have been able to return the onesie seconds after she bought it, which is probably true. *But.* She's hitting a roadblock, and she is stuck in that moment in time. She can't see her way clear to any other possible solution.

"I was so upset. How could they not give me a refund? It wasn't like I spilled a strawberry margarita on the damn thing! I just changed my mind," Florence says.

"I could go for a strawberry margarita about now," says Kevin, knitting his striped sock.

"Or a banana daiquiri. You know with like a little umbrella in it? And, like, chunks of ice or whatever?" says Jojo.

This is what happens when you get a bunch of Canadian knitters together in the dead of winter. Tropical drink envy. I should have brought some mango juice and a blender. Would have kept everyone happy and killed a half hour.

"I get that you were upset, Florence, and I don't blame you. What next?" I ask.

"Nothing. I walked out, went to the Hallmark store, bought the most darling Winnie-the-Pooh gift bag and matching tissue paper with little Eeyores on it, and then—"

"For ninety-three bucks they wouldn't even gift-wrap it for you?" Lauren wants to know.

"I didn't ask them to. The first time I walked out I was thinking about the onesie and whether I made the right decision. The second time I walked out furious that the clerk wouldn't give me my money back. I don't understand what was in her head."

"It's so hard to get good help in retail these days," says Lauren.

"Some bosses are also totally bait,"* Jojo says. "My old boss used to, like, count the cash to make sure we weren't stealing or whatever."

Um, that's a normal business practice, Jojo. But not everything has to be a teaching moment. I gently steer us back to the topic.

"We can speculate about the motives of the cashier. Was she trying to stick to the policy? Was she interpreting the rules too strictly? Would the owner of the shop have handled things differently? These are all excellent questions," I say.

I see smiles and heads nodding.

"But they are all irrelevant."

I explain to the knitters that we are getting off track. To

---

*   *Bait* is slang for "terrible."

get Florence's voice heard in this situation she needs to keep focused. Rather than attempt to understand the motives of the clerk at the boutique, Florence should have shifted her thinking immediately into compromise mode. When we don't get what we want on the first try, sometimes we are able to work our way into compromises that would fulfill the same agenda. It's up to us to ask for what we want, and if we can't get what we want (in this case, cold, hard cash), we ask for what we are willing to settle for (suggestions follow).

For example, instead of a refund, Florence could have asked for a gift card in exchange. Although she wouldn't get her money back, she would at least get "credit" with her family for the amount she spent. Also, the new mommy would have been able to choose any fancy pair of pants that she wanted. But to get this, Florence would have had to use her voice to ask for it.

Or Florence could have requested an over-the-top gift-wrapping job, with silver paper and matching ribbons cascading down. High-end boutiques often stock shiny boxes and bags that look ultra-chic for a baby shower where your gifts are on display — and, let's face it, up for judgment by all the other guests. I am a little sad that this delicate, hand-embroidered piece of clothing ended up nestled in wrapping paper festooned with depressed donkeys, but then again, Winnie-the-Pooh has always rubbed me the wrong way.

Another option would be to ask the salesperson/cashier to throw in another item, just to make the present appear more robust. For example, a handmade baby toy to compliment the onesie, or a pair of matching socks and a hairband with a poppy on it. Possibly the young cashier doesn't have the authority to add anything to the gift. Also possible that the store is owned by her mom, and she has all the authority in the world. We won't know unless we ask. We can all agree that ninety-three dollars is an insane amount of money to spend on what is essentially a fancy undershirt for a six-month-old, so the store must on some level know that they are being unreasonable, and therefore be willing to compromise. The clerk may be empowered to do just that.

"Florence, listen to me. Sounds like you were trying to do the right thing here by buying something kind of spendy for your sister-in-law's new grandbaby."

She nods.

I continue. "Sometimes we try things, and they don't work out 100 percent as planned."

Jojo lifts up her hoodie to show us a tattoo of what is either a wolf in heat or a map of Maine. "Tell me about it," she says.

"If you turn a complaint transaction into an all-or-nothing game — like, either I get my money back or I'm leaving, then you're the one who will lose everything," I explain. "Even if she was sticking to the policy like Gorilla Glue, maybe the cashier would have been willing to not-so-discreetly tuck in a copy of the receipt so that the baby's mom could see how much you spent. But once you turn it into a win-lose? That hand-embroidered onesie is all ya got, and you're back in the parking lot trying to remember where you parked your car."

Ideally, the cashier would offer a few choices. But if she doesn't, as in this case, you need to be the one to suggest alternatives. Don't get so stuck on the injustice being committed that you miss your chance to get something else equally useful.

Like, for example, you might have to tap-dance for two and a half hours at the knitting store, but at least you'll have a great story to tell. And you'll be paid in yarn.

Questions for Reflection

1. Sometimes we get locked into a yes/no battle and forget to compromise. Does this ever happen to you? Why or why not? How can you remind yourself to look at the bigger picture? Which techniques would work for you?

2. Part of this problem was that Florence was afraid of her sister-in-law's judgment of her gift. We are all guilty of occasional judgment and the fear of judgment. Which is more likely to happen to you? Think about what role you play in gift-giving judgment. Is there an opportunity to be more kind? Can you make a difference in someone's world?

3. The owner of the knitting store was surely looking at this problem differently than the others. As a small-business owner, she saw the perspective of the invisible onesie store owner and how difficult it is to keep good customers as well as to retain decent staff. Choose a situation that you have been "stuck with," and think of people with different perspectives from your own. Gently ask one of them if they would be willing to listen to your issue and give some advice. It might be interesting to see your problem from a completely different point of view.

How to Report a Rhyming Physician or Other Health-Care Professional

Consider Your Timing

I am in a stranger's living room in a suburban apartment complex. Older couples sit on folding chairs and listen to my lecture about complaining. Last month they had a dentist showing slides of his safari in Tanzania. It's a Wednesday evening in 2014, and I have just started public speaking about complaining effectively, so I take any gig I can get. As the talk draws to an end, I open the floor for questions. Gertrude, a blonde woman of a certain age, is the first to put down her coffee cup and raise her hand. She looks upset before she even starts talking.

"Seventeen years ago, my husband got sick. We were in the hospital, waiting for the specialist to come in. My husband was shivering in a paper gown, and I was a nervous wreck. The doctor came in and introduced himself. He said, 'My name is Dr. Rittler, rhymes with Hitler.'"*

The room went quiet. You could hear the sound of people feeling sad.

"Oh, Gertrude. That must have been so tough. What did you say?" I ask.

"We didn't say a word. We were so shocked," she says.

"I agree. That is a really odd way to introduce yourself."

"Especially for us," Gertrude says. "My husband's father was hidden in a barn during World War II. He subsisted on straw and water for years. He met my mother-in-law after, and she always swore he smelled a bit horsey. We were both brought up to never talk about those times, and to never, ever, *ever* say the H-word."

"What happened when you told the doctor that?" I want to know.

"We didn't," she says.

"Oh. So, who did you tell? What did you do?" I ask.

She looks at me like I am a bit thick. "We didn't do anything. It was such a disgusting way to introduce yourself and such a sickening way to act, we couldn't even respond. A few weeks after that, my husband passed away. And every night I think about that awful doctor, and his horrific introduction. I haven't slept through the night in seventeen years."

Gertrude, I'm sorry for your loss. But hold on a second. Not sleeping for over a decade? Because of the stupid comment of

---

* Everyone in the story's name has been changed, but the integrity of the story has been preserved.

a complete stranger? That's a classic example of why complaining is so important. Because Gertrude kept her mouth shut, this offhand introduction was able to grow and grow in her mind until it became bigger than what actually happened. I'm no therapist, but from where I'm sitting, it looks like she has now confused this dumb remark with the tragic illness and subsequent death of her husband.

"What should I have done?" Gertrude asks.

"Well, first, I would have probably let the doctor know that this was an insensitive introduction. Maybe something like, 'I'm sure you didn't know this, but we're descendants of Holocaust survivors, and the H-word is very disturbing for us,'" I suggest. Chances are this physician had no idea the extent to which some people are offended by the name Hitler, and had he known, he might not have used it.

"I couldn't have said that," Gertrude says. "We were way too upset, and I was brought up to believe that the doctor is always right. Even if I had wanted to say something, the words would have stuck in my throat. What else could we have done?"

I can understand Gertrude's point. If she didn't want to say anything directly to the specialist, what else could she have done?

She could have complained to the clinic manager on the way out. If she didn't want to address the clinic staff in person, she could have called later that afternoon, asked to speak to someone in charge of patient relations, and explained what happened and why it was particularly upsetting to her and her family. Even if Gertrude waited a week or two, her complaint still would have been relevant to someone at the hospital or the clinic, and I'm pretty sure the doctor would have been spoken to about more appropriate introductions. Or she could have sent an email. Or if the option was available, she could have filled out a survey (online or on paper, whatever they had) to express her dissatisfaction. I am not normally a fan of anonymous complaints, but in this case, even a note in the clinic's suggestion box would have been better than saying nothing at all.

The other choice Gertrude had was to report the physician to a higher authority. The exact office varies widely by county, state, and country. In most places, doctors report to a professional order that accepts complaints regarding their treatment of clients and their behavior. This incident was disturbing enough that I think it could have risen to the level of a formal complaint.

Although it's true that the comment couldn't be erased once said, the doctor should have been told about this for several reasons. First, Gertrude might have been able to let go of the issue had she dealt with it immediately or shortly thereafter. Second, had the doctor been told about it, he could have come up with another snappy introduction and not gone around continuing to potentially insult people with his H-word rhyming scheme. Third, if the doctor did not have the best intentions, at least there would have been a record of his actions so that when the next person complained, it would be the second infraction and therefore taken more seriously than the first.

Taking your time and phrasing a complaint is understandable, but taking time and never coming forward just causes problems that could have been solved had you addressed them at the time. I read a study about why patients don't always complain when they are dissatisfied, and it concluded that, in most cases, it comes down to communication: "The evidence that is available has clearly identified that a significant number of reported incidents of concern have resulted from communication failures." And in my opinion, not communicating is the biggest failure of all.

When people are stressed or nervous about their complaint, I always tell them to take their time, breathe, and gather their thoughts. I believe that the effectiveness of the complaint grows as you begin to calm down. Depending on what the issue is, the complaint may be able to wait until you're ready. In some situations, it's more important to appear calm and get all your points across than to be immediate and flustered.

Waiting till you're ready implies that at a certain point you will bring your concerns forward and attempt to get them remedied. The saddest stories to me are the ones where people hold in their complaints, and they fester until the memory of what happened becomes much bigger than the original issue.

I'm sorry for Gertrude that her husband passed away and that the end of his life was fraught with complicated emotions brought on by interactions like this one. I urge all of you to get into the habit of speaking up so that when something particularly hurtful occurs you will already have practice, and it won't be so difficult to determine whom to talk to and what to say.

Moment of Silence

In deference to the seriousness of this complaint, I will not close this chapter with a joke, but rather with a moment of silence for the twelve million people, six million Jews, and about one hundred family members that I myself lost in the Holocaust.

Thank you.

How to Get a Ski Jacket Repaired without a Receipt, and Also Return a Coffeemaker

Two Stories with the Same Ending

Story One

My first ombudsman office had a glass window to the left of my desk that overlooked a beautiful courtyard that no one ever used.

I was staring out the window one late afternoon, watching a little bird hop around in the snow, when it occurred to me that in addition to listening to complaints all day, I could be writing about them and helping people solve their problems. Because I had no track record as a writer, I set my sights low and cold-called a local free paper. During that first call, I pitched them an "Ask the Ombudsman" column where people could write in with their complaining problems and I would give advice. They agreed immediately, which caused me to wonder if I had aimed too low and should have gone for a more prestigious media outlet, but then again, a bird in the hand is better than one flitting around outside your window.

The current wrench in the works was that complaints were not flowing in. In fact, we were receiving no mail at all. I decided to solve this problem by wandering up and down the halls of the office in the hope that the usual small talk with coworkers would produce material for my column. One particularly freezing day I saw Lynnie heading off to the parking lot with her ski jacket unzipped.

We rejoin the action as a blizzard swirls overhead, and wind blows through the thin glass doors.

"Lynnie! Do up your coat before you go outside!" I say. Lynnie is in the lobby, getting in a few deep knee lunges before she heads to her car.

"Wish I could," she says, lifting her arms over her head to show me the broken zipper. "This happened at the ski hill over the weekend, and now I can't do it up."

"You skied this weekend? It was minus 35 up north," I say, focusing on the rugged Canadian attitude and missing the fact that here was a potential complaint column unfolding under my nose.

"Can't stand being trapped in the house for two days," she says, stretching her calf muscles.

"Oh, right, yeah, me neither," I lie, thinking longingly of my jammies, couch, remote control, *People* magazine, knitting, and stack of mystery novels.*

"How did the zipper break?" I ask. Did it get caught on the

---

* My auntie Marcy gave me a subscription to *People* magazine for my thirteenth birthday, and she renews it every year, much to my delight and appreciation.

gondola as she pirouetted out the door? Did it tear on a jump while she flipped her G3 skis?

"My husband and I were stuck on the chairlift for a while, and he reached into my uh, well, um, my zipper got stuck, and er—"

I don't know Lynnie well enough to ask any more questions. In fact, I don't know her well enough to tell her to zip up her jacket in the first place.

"This jacket cost more than my skis. I only got to wear it twice. I wanted to bring it back, but I can't find the receipt. I looked in my gym bag, my swimming backpack, my ballet case, and my canoeing sack. Nothing."

"Did you look with your ski stuff?" I ask.

"Of course! Tried my ski stuff, snowboarding gear, and Ski-Doo suit. Found some trail mix, hot paw packs, and a coupon for Nuru massage.* No receipt. Now I'm going to have to spend the whole winter with my jacket open. How will I play women's snowflake rugby?"†

"You know this problem might be solvable, right?" I offer. "You may be able to get the jacket repaired even without a proof of purchase."

"Seriously? How would that work?" she asks.

Here's what I suggest: "Take the jacket back to the boutique at the ski hill where you got it. Show them that the zipper broke and needs to be repaired. Explain that you bought it from them, but you can't find the receipt. Be honest. If you

---

* Nuru is when the masseuse (a woman) oils up her entire body and massages the client by rubbing up against him or her. It's as risqué as it sounds.
† Not a real sport. I made it up.

bought it last year at the end of the season, tell them. If you paid full price for it a few weeks ago, tell them."

I suggest telling the truth for several reasons. First, integrity. Your word is all you have; you need to know that you have the self-respect to be honest. Second, they may be able to search for the transaction based on your credit card. If you lie about when you got the jacket, one of two things will happen: either they will find the receipt in the computer and you will feel stupid for lying, or you will have to add new lies to cover your tracks (e.g., "I don't have my credit card," "I forgot that I bought it a few weeks ago," etc.), and that will be more complicated to remember and/or manage. Third, there may be something unique about your jacket that makes it traceable even without the credit card, and you have no idea. Maybe it was the last one in that size? Maybe it was the last one in that color combination? The people in the store might remember the jacket and have information regarding when it was bought and sold that could be incriminating if you tried to hide it. Finally, I have believed for a while that people can tell if you're lying, and it makes them less likely to help you.

If you spend serious money on a piece of clothing such as a ski jacket, the boutique should be willing to stand behind their merchandise. I would try to get them to repair it before I would demand an exchange or refund. Some of these boutique-type stores have deals with seamstresses to fix things that tear or break in the normal course of business. Larger department stores might have an in-house tailor that can make smaller repairs, especially if they are dealing with a high-end purchase.

When she gets to the customer service desk, Lynnie can tell them about her plans to climb snowy mountains and skate across icy rivers this winter, none of which would be safe with a jacket that does not zip up. If it were my jacket, I would be stuck telling them about my trek from my parked car to my front door. Less impactful. You may want to mention your planned polar bear photography expedition, outdoor camping s'mores bake-off, or cross-country ski marathon.*

In any event, the store should be willing to pay for a repair for a brand-new jacket that was more expensive than a hot-stone massage at an exclusive spa. If the store manager or other clerk is not in favor of paying for your jacket repair, they may still be able to refer you to someone who is an expert in executing this kind of work. That wouldn't be as good as getting it for free, but you would still know that your jacket would be fixed by an expert.

If the person helping you is actually a helpful person but knows nothing about zipper repair, you can ask them if you could exchange the jacket for one with a working zipper or for a different brand that does not have a defective zipper. They may have a policy where they can take things back without a receipt. Or they may be willing to ignore their "No Refunds / No Exchange" policy just to give good customer service.

If the person helping you is not actually helpful, I would suggest leaving with the jacket and coming back another day to try your luck on a return or exchange. Remember Florence, the knitter with the baby gift on page 45? Her case was slightly different than this one for the following reasons:

- Lynnie's jacket is broken and needs to be repaired. There is nothing wrong with the onesie, other than its price.

---

* Choose the one closest to the truth.

- Florence changed her mind immediately. Lynnie is coming back weeks later.
- Lynnie doesn't have her receipt. Ink on Florence's receipt was not yet dry.

Also, the onesie purchase was time-sensitive — it was needed for a baby shower, so the buyer didn't have the luxury of returning to try another approach. With Lynnie's broken zipper, winter is already well under way, so a few days here or there will not make a huge difference.

A few weeks after this lengthy — and freezing — conversation, I bump into Lynnie in the parking lot. Her tuque is pulled down, her fleece scarf is wrapped tightly — and her jacket is zipped to her neck.

"Your jacket is zipped! What happened?" I ask.

"I took your advice, and it more than worked! I brought my jacket to the little shop at the ski hill. I showed them the broken zipper, and I asked where they thought I could get it repaired, and guess what?"

"They gave you the name of a tailor? They had a sewing machine on-site? Little bluebirds swooped down to fix the zipper?"

"Ha-ha. Nope," Lynnie says. "They took a look at the broken zipper and offered me a brand-new coat. They are the exclusive distributors of this brand in Quebec, so even without the receipt, they knew it had come from their store."

This is great. "Can I take your picture and use it for this week's column?" I ask.

Lynnie blushes. "Do you have to? Can't you just take a pic of the jacket?"

And that's what I did. Despite her courageous ice-climbing and heli-skiing abilities, and the gumption she had to ask for repairs on a broken jacket without a receipt, when it comes to having her picture taken, Lynnie is more of a chicken than a bald eagle.

The lessons learned here are that even if you are not 100 percent in the right, sometimes it might be worth a try to get what you want and need. Also, you don't always have to come on aggressively with your biggest ask (new jacket). You can start smaller (jacket repair), and work your way up to the bigger demand depending on how the conversation is going. Finally, if you feel the conversation is not going anywhere, you can leave the store and try your luck with someone else. And, if you are looking out the window and see a bird flailing around, pay attention — it may be trying to lead you to a bigger story.

Story Two

I already mentioned to you that this book was acquired by someone named Georgia, whom I've only met over the phone but seems lovely, and whom I really want to keep happy because she is giving me the chance to write and publish so that I can talk to all of you about how to stand up for yourselves. Plus, I'd like to possibly convince her to take more of my future books, including the one I want to write about basketball that my friend Riana has tentatively titled *Dribble*.

I gave you an example that came up during our first phone call about the airline seats reclining. And in the interest of satisfying the needs of all concerned, I imagined how that would go and how you could speak to someone who was backing their seat into your personal space when you had cash-flow reports to submit as soon as your flight landed.

One or two calls later, Georgia told me about her experience complaining effectively and how she achieved good results. It's similar to the ski jacket story, so I am pairing them together for maximum impact.

A few months ago, Georgia had a houseguest. He generously purchased for her and her family a complex coffeemaker that also chopped liver and minced onions. Just kidding. That's a Yiddish expression for an appliance that does everything. This coffeemaker does not mince onions (although it probably could). It grinds beans and steams milk and does everything coffee-related, including taking up an inordinate amount of space on the kitchen countertop. For these reasons, it remained in its box for several months.*

The hosts were reluctant to attempt to return the coffeemaker because it was so big and so heavy to get in and out of the car, plus they had no receipt, not even a gift receipt or a stray piece of store wrapping paper, and at this point several months had elapsed.

Houseguest comes back to stay and notices the unopened box next to the sofa in the basement. Georgia and husband are temporarily mortified because they think Houseguest is going to be offended that they never opened the coffee roaster/brewer/steamer.

In fact, Houseguest is not upset at all. "If you aren't going to use the coffeemaker, let's bring it back!" he says. "I'll help you. We can bring it back to the store after the, uh, Sanka."†

Sounds like a plan.

---

*   I had guests for dinner this weekend, and the family of five brought…absolutely nothing. No wine, no pie, no box of chocolates. Not even a six-pack and a bag of chips from the gas station down the street. I'm a little bitter about Georgia's coffeemaker.

†   Sanka is a brand of instant decaf coffee that comes in an orange package and was big in the early '80s. Many think it is making a comeback because of its retro appeal.

They rent a moving truck, hire six movers to hoist the box up, and head to the big box store. Kidding. It's big but not that big. They get the box into the trunk of the car and close it with bungee cords. Maybe you have driven past them on the highway? *Joking again.* They pile into the car, with the coffeemaker, and head to the strip mall. They carry the coffeemaker in past the front doors and put it on the customer service counter, where mercifully there is no line.

The woman behind the counter looks at the sealed box and asks for the receipt. Georgia says that she doesn't have a receipt; it was a gift from a generous houseguest, who only stayed the weekend but went above and beyond, not only with this gift but also with fresh flowers. The guest even stripped the bed before they left and put their used towels in the pillowcase on the floor. Woman behind the counter nods approvingly and keys some numbers into the cash register. Houseguest puffs out his chest a little bit, feeling appreciated.

"I'm afraid I can't help you without a receipt," she says.

Houseguest unpuffs.

Husband looks at Georgia as if to say, "I knew this was a bad idea. I could be home watching football."

Georgia responds with her eyes, saying, "Hang on, it's not over yet."

Woman behind the counter puts her hands on the box and sighs. "There's really nothing I can do for you. Other than an exchange."

"An exchange?" they ask, perking up.

"Well, it doesn't have to be a straight exchange. I can give you a gift card for the full amount, and you can use it anytime," woman behind the counter says.

Georgia is delighted. This is even better than she imagined. A gift, generous but bulky and not needed, has been sitting in its box next to the sofa, playing the role of an extra coffee table. Now, it is about to become a slender little gift card with several hundred dollars on it.

Her husband is thinking they may be able to do even better. She can sense that he's about to ask for a cash refund, instead of a gift card. She intercepts the ball before he can catch it, and suggests that he take a walk over to the big-screen TVs and catch a score while the gift card is being processed.

He takes the hint and wanders off with Houseguest.

Georgia slips the gift card into her wallet.

The hardest part of this complaint was initiating the return process. It was difficult to get the box into the store for several reasons. First, the physical size and discomfort of having to transport the coffeemaker made it a more-than-one-person job, which meant that schedules had to coordinate. Second, once a full week had passed, and then another week, and then another week, the box tended to blend into the decor, and getting rid of it seemed less urgent. Third, the further away anyone is from the purchase date, the less likely they usually are to do a successful return. We can talk ourselves out of potentially embarrassing situations, convincing ourselves that the clerk will laugh at us or will ask personal questions (such as "How could you not want this coffeemaker? It's fantastic," or "Why didn't you return it sooner? This is an older model"). True, that could happen, but more likely, the people behind the counter are focused on doing their jobs — processing returns and satisfying customers and punching in their time sheets. It is unlikely that they are stopping to consider what motivated you to return your coffee contraption today. We all hear voices of judgment, and we have to learn not to let them stop us from trying to get what we need — in this case a fully loaded gift card.

This situation has a few things in common with the ski jacket story. First, both are retail complaints. Second, in both cases a lot of money was spent purchasing something that fell short of expectation — either because the zipper broke or because it was a gift that didn't really suit the lifestyle. Third, both stories are about bringing something back to the store without a receipt and being honest and straightforward when explaining what happened. Finally, in both cases the outcomes depend on the attitude of the person behind the counter, and both end positively.

The lessons learned are that you never know if a return is going to work unless you try it. Even if you don't have the receipt, you can still try your best to get your money back or your coat fixed.

Alternate Universe Analysis

In both of these scenarios, the store clerks were clearly empowered to help customers. But what if you go into the ski chalet shop and ask for a jacket repair and the clerk says, "No. You don't have a receipt. I have no way of knowing whether or not you bought the jacket here, and therefore I can't offer you access to our private and exclusive repair service."

You can't really argue because, technically, you're in the wrong. You don't have proof that you bought the jacket there, and, in addition, you broke the zipper. So now the best you can do is try to get your garment repaired by an expert. You can ask questions about their tailoring service with the ultimate goal of finding out who can properly repair the jacket zipper without damaging the jacket, even if you have to pay for it. You might ask who they use and if that tailor has a retail location and/or a website.

If they won't give you any assistance, you have one card left to play: You may be able to look up the manufacturer online and contact them directly. This could look like a phone call or email explaining your situation and asking for advice regarding repair options, or asking to return the jacket. If you have tried everything you can think of, you can always box up the jacket with an explanatory letter and send it back to the company. You may get a replacement or a refund, or you may get nothing. Well, nothing material, but at least you'll have the satisfaction of knowing that you knocked on every possible door.

The coffeemaker situation, in contrast, doesn't easily lend itself to shipping back to the manufacturer because of its size and weight. If the store clerk will not exchange or refund your gargantuan box, you can push a little harder and say something like "As you can see, this box is super big and heavy. I'm really not excited to carry it back to the car and schlep it home. Anything you can give me for it would be much appreciated."

Even if they still refuse to help you, you have the option of leaving the box there, and although you won't have any financial gain, at least you'll have cleared your house of a large eyesore.

If you don't want to leave the box there, you can try to sell the appliance using a website or app (or if you have teenagers like I do, get *them* to sell it; they seem to know all about online marketplaces). You can also drop it off at the Salvation Army or any thrift store in your neighborhood. You don't need to find a perfect match for it (e.g., "I wonder if the SPCA can use a coffeemaker?"). I have confidence that large umbrella

organizations like Goodwill are capable of managing dona-
tions and finding homes for them.

Finally, it must be said that the best way to avoid this kind
of situation is to hold on to your receipt. Put it in a file, take
a picture of it, tape it to the box. Find a system that works for
you so that you won't ever have to worry about whether your
end table is returnable.

10

How to Find a Unicorn Frappuccino

Listen for Clues

Starbucks came out with a Unicorn Frappuccino. It's pink. It's also purple. (It changes colors.) It's sweet. It's also tart. (It changes flavors.) Remember the story about returning the giant and unwieldy coffee machine? I used the expression "It also chops liver and minces onions." That would be applicable here too. Not because the Uni Frapp actually chops liver but because it changes color and flavor, which is so unusual that a cynical person might wonder what else this beverage is capable of.

The drink has whipped cream with powdered pink-and-purple candy sprinkled on top. The circulating theory is that this drink was designed for Instagram and teenage girls, and that's how the colors were selected and the powders were designed. I could make it sound to you like I'm only in this story for my kids, but in the interest of authenticity I will admit that

I'm disproportionately attracted to bright and sparkly things, especially those that are on trend.

Unicorn Frappuccinos are available for a limited time only — like less than a week. Clearly the intent is to have a big bang, and then disappear before anyone actually bothers to taste the thing. The Frappuccinos are available till Sunday. Today is Saturday, so this shouldn't be a problem.

My daughter Liberty and I stop at the Starbucks in our neighborhood. They are sold out of Uni Frapps. *Huh.* I was ready for the overpriced drink, the oversweet taste, and the potential for overdosing on social media likes, but it didn't occur to me that the drink would actually sell out. Thankfully, Starbucks retail locations are not hard to come by.

I have raised my children to be resourceful. I often say that if they were in a flood (God forbid), they would be the three people clinging to that one roof shingle as the water flowed by. I did not anticipate the application of this skill to sussing out Starbucks's latest, but hey, I'm also hoping for a Unicorn Frappuccino at this point. Twelve-year-old Liberty gets back in my car and starts looking up Starbucks locations, and calling to see if they have Unicorn Frappuccinos, which, according to the hype, are supposed to be available for at least the next twenty-four hours.

She is getting the following answers: "Nope," "No," and "Are you kidding me?" Turns out unicorns are as elusive as we have always been led to believe.

She hatches the following plan: "Mom, will you take me to Plattsburgh?" Like I said, these folks are resourceful.

Plattsburgh is in New York State. We live in Canada. She wants us not only to cross state lines but also to drive to another country, just to put fifty-nine grams of sugar — adorable sugar — into her prepubescent system. This will involve an hour-plus drive, a stop at the border, an interrogation at Customs. I can just see it now:

"Where ya headed today, ma'am?" the guy will say.

"Looking for a, um, unicorn. Unicorn Frappuccino," I will answer.

"Pull over to the side, ma'am, and please step out of your vehicle."

I will be publicly humiliated. Accused of chasing the Loch Ness Monster! Bigfoot! Unicorns! Alternatively, and possibly even worse, the border agent will be a fellow conspiracy theorist. He will wink at us and slip the card for his UFO club into my passport. "Catch you on the flip side," he'll say meaningfully, hand on his belt buckle. Imaginary scenarios are getting worse.

On the other hand, life is for the living! We have passports! While we may not be jetting off to Paris on a moment's notice, that doesn't mean we can't hightail it down the highway to upstate New York. We have time! We have a car!

We can go tomorrow.

But before we leave the country to throw hard-earned cash at a greedy multinational — even one with fantastic pink drinks — we should probably call first.

"HithisisStarbucksPlattsburghweareallsoldoutofUnicorn-FrappuccinoshowmayIhelpyou?" says the barista answering the phone.

Oh.

It's 2:30 p.m., and we are planning to visit my great-aunt and -uncle at 3 p.m.[*]

---

[*]   Yes, this great-aunt and great-uncle are the same ones that I disappointed at the 5k race, on page 13.

It's time to entertain the possibility that we will not be getting Unicorn Frappuccinos. We may have to drown our sorrows in one of the other off-menu beverages, which if it's any consolation, I'm sure also has fifty-nine grams of sugar. Also, when we began this quest, we promised my oldest and vegan-for-now son, B,* that we are going on a Starbucks run, and he is probably still jonesing for a vegan Frappuccino, unicorns notwithstanding.

We go home to get B, and together we all hit up another Starbucks in the neighborhood that has already told us they don't have Uni Frapps. It's best that B order his own drink; in my experience, vegans sometimes need a little extra TLC to get their almond soy coconut situations sorted.

"Mom, this tastes kind of funny; it's not sweet enough," B says. "I need them to make me a new one."

"They probably stopped after sugar spoonful number 57," I mumble. By now, I have spent more time searching for, not finding, and consoling the loss of Unicorn Frappuccinos than it probably took them to come up with the concept. I am running out of patience.

He brings the drink back to the barista — remember, clinging to that one roof shingle. They make him a new one.

"It still tastes kind of funny, Mom, and not like I need them to make me a new one or whatever, but they shouldn't be selling these to, like, other vegans or, like, other customers, so I need to say something," B says.

Why, oh why, oh why, why, why, do I let my children read my work? Yes, complaining effectively is important. And yes, I want you to stand up for all the other non-animal-product

---

* His real name is Ezra, but I call him B. My other son is named Benji, but I call him Beno, pronounced Ben-o or Benno.

consumers in line behind you. But does it really have to be now?

I don't say any of that. I take my iced coffee and Liberty's vanilla crème something and two hot chocolates for my great-aunt and -uncle, and we go wait in the car.

Fifteen minutes elapse.

B comes out juggling multiple (well, at least two) vegan drinks, and pours a bit of this into some of that until he has exactly the right mix of Frappuccino, which frankly seems just as complicated as the Unicorn, though it is neither pink nor purple.

We go visit my aunt and uncle and bring them hot chocolate with whip.

We apologize for not bringing Unicorn Frappuccinos. First, we explain what Unicorn Frappuccinos are. They are intrigued. They are the type of ninety-year-olds that have iPads and read a lot of news. We discuss the merits of a limited-time offer. We wonder if the drink really does change color as promised. We show them videos of the alleged color change.

We sip our non-Unicorn non-Frappuccinos and agree that the purple and pink drinks are probably too sweet. Probably undrinkable, in fact. Other than a few snapshots, they are definitely not worth the $7.95 everyone is paying for them.

"Wait," B says. "They have Unicorn Frappuccinos downtown across from the Bell Centre."

Four pairs of eyes turn to look at him. Why is he just telling us this now, in my great-aunt and -uncle's living room? Where was he during the Great Starbucks Scavenger Hunt of fifteen minutes ago?

"How do you know?" my uncle asks.

B answers as follows: "Well, while I was in there having my vegan drink remade for the third time, I heard the baristas talking. They said there was one location in the city that still had th—"

Before his sentence is even finished, Liberty is on the phone to the barista—

Just kidding.

Before she is even off the phone, we peel away from the curb, tires squealing.

We head right to the store across from the Bell Centre, and lo and behold! The insider information was correct. It is the last retail outlet in the Montreal metropolitan area to carry the powdered purple-and-pink sugar necessary to concoct the sweet confection known to all humanity and most tweenage girls as the Unicorn Frappuccino.

We buy two, share one, and bring the other back to my great-aunt and -uncle's house for them to see and enjoy. They save it for dessert that night and proclaim it a little too sweet but definitely interesting.

There are many lessons to be learned from this story. I'm going to give you a few to start with:

- Sometimes you might be willing to travel to great lengths, like to upstate New York, when what you are looking for is actually available right next door, which is a lesson also learned by Dorothy in *The Wizard of Oz.**
- If you're vegan, and you drink Frappuccinos, you will have access to information that the rest of us couldn't pay for even if we wanted to.
- If you have your drink remade multiple times, the baristas

---

* I was at a story slam this summer, and one of the talks was by the grand-daughter of the actor who played the Cowardly Lion (Bert Lahr) in the original *Wizard of Oz*, so you are now less than six degrees of separation from the whole cast.

will "accidentally" leak top-secret-classified corporate information to you just to get you out of their store.
- Although we are all sad that the Canadiens lost the play-
  offs, the Bell Centre is still good for something.*

I told you this story because I think it's funny, and also
because I believe it's the best one in my repertoire to illustrate
the concept of keeping your ears and eyes open when it comes
to asking for what you want. Here we are, driving around to
different locations, all of which are telling us there are no UFs
to be had in the city. We call a store in another country that has
also sold out. No one is offering assistance or suggesting we go
downtown. The only reason we found out that might work is
because B was listening to the baristas talk to each other while
they made his drink. He may have been paying attention to
make sure they didn't add cow pus (vegan term for milk), but
in the end, his insider intelligence was helpful to us in getting
what we want (not necessarily need).

However, my son overhearing the conversation makes
me realize that we could have possibly had the same results
by walking into the store and asking a million questions. We
could have encouraged the baristas to start talking among
themselves about the elusive Frappuccinos, and maybe someone would have mentioned that they were still available near
the Bell Centre. I believe this technique is much more effective
in person than on the phone, where it's a lot easier to say, "I
don't know," and hang up.

The subplot about B having his drink remade is a tough
one. On the one hand, if your beverage does not taste right, I

---

* The Canadiens are the Montreal hockey team, who had a rough time
  in the spring of 2016 when this story takes place. They play at the Bell
  Centre downtown.

support you asking to have it remade. On the other hand, the third, eleventh, or sixteenth time you have an issue with your drink, I begin to wonder if it's you. Also, as the person *waiting* for the person having their cappuccino refoamed or reheated or restirred, it is sometimes difficult to have patience. If the person unhappy with their drink asked my advice, I would say, "Absolutely have it remade. You are a paying customer, and you should not accept a drink with brown lettuce."* If the person remaking the drink were to come to me for help, I would say, "It's okay to set limits. You don't have to remake a drink seven, eight, or eleven times. After the second or third — depending on your patience and company policy — you can gently tell the customer that you have nothing more to offer drink-wise, and this really is the best you can do." For the person waiting, I would say that they are under no obligation to wait an un-limited amount of time for a drink to be remixed. They can set their own limits, and wait in the car as I did, or, if this is a recurring pattern that they have had enough of, maybe offer to meet back another time.

When looking for something elusive like a deal with a short promotion window, I suggest you ask to get your vegan drink remade three times. Just kidding. I would argue that you would be able to get similar information by asking as many questions as possible. The key is to do so in person. When we were calling around, we asked if they knew of any places that might have Uni Frapps, and every person who answered said they had no idea. When you call, you only get the answers from whoever picks up the phone. In person, you can hear the responses of all the baristas (or whatever applies to your situation). Listen

---

* If you are reading this book in order, it makes perfect sense.

to the answers, listen to the clerks talking, and see if you can collect more data about this deal and the best way to access it.

Seeing this problem from all sides tells us that there is no right or wrong answer. Everyone can set their own limits and communicate what they are before a real conflict occurs. Also let your friends know that you are fussy about your Starbucks and might have to send it back. Let your clients know that you can only repour three times before your patience expires, and so on.

When Else to Use This Technique

Let's say you are scrolling through your social media feed, and you click on an advertised deal for cropped hoodies, but when you check the website the hoodie is not there. Before you give up, look around the internet and see if you can find out more info about these adorable zip-crops, beginning with but not limited to the main seller's website. You can also look at relevant influencers, fan blogs, company Snapchat/Instagram stories — anyone anywhere who may have insider information about this deal. You can post questions or @ them (which means message the influencers directly) to ask where you can get the coupon code you need or the sale link you are looking for. This is not the same as lurking around a store, but it's another way to get people talking, and glean whatever information you can.

11

How to Get Your Log-In ID and Password to Function Correctly

Stay on It

My book club friend who lives across the street has a nephew staying with her who is teaching business classes at Concordia University, where I am the ombudsperson.[*] She tells me that he is enjoying the work, particularly his business communications classes. He teaches four of them, and now that she thinks of it, he does a section on complaining, and she should introduce us.

"That really is a coincidence," I tell her, "because last year, or two years ago, that class was taught by a mom in my former karate carpool, and she invited me to guest-lecture."

A few weeks later I get an email inviting me to teach a section at each of these classes, which I graciously accept.

---

[*] My book club has been together for almost fifteen years. We meet once a month, have a holiday gift exchange in December, and are closed to new members. The only thing is — we barely read books.

It's interesting how each section of the class will take on its own personality, even when taught by the same prof. The first group I met was very concerned about the fairness of grading on a curve and how curves were applied. They asked many technical questions relating to As, Bs, Cs, and the fairness of allocating each. A few students in the second group worked in customer service, and they were interested in talking about what customer service agents can actually do to solve problems. They were fascinated to discover the variation in the amount of power between customer service jobs at different companies. I don't remember Group Three very well because I was burning up with fever and had no business being at work that day, much less guest-lecturing a bunch of innocent (and healthy) students. It was poor judgment on my part, and I apologize.

Which brings us to Group Four.

I finish my slide deck, take a sip of my Tim Horton's coffee, and open the floor to questions. A guy with long blond hair and black-rimmed glasses raises his hand. We never learn his name but he looks like a Dylan, so let's go with that.

"What do you do if a company says they're going to fix something, but don't?" Dylan asks.

"I need more detail; please keep going," I say, and look to the instructor for confirmation that I have enough time. He nods and takes a sip of his grande extra hot latte.* We clearly pass different coffee shops on our way to this building.

"Well, I was trying to play *Downward Spiral: Horus Station*

---

*   Hey, Encyclopedia Brown, there is no way for me to know what's in his cup. I am just signaling to you that it's from Starbucks and taking some poetic license.

on my Xbox, and I couldn't log on," he says. He explains that he bought the video game and was able to set up his log-in and password on his computer, but when he tried to log in on his game console, the screen froze.

"Is that typical?" I ask. I know nothing about video games.

"No. First time I've had that problem. I powered down, powered back up. Nothing," Dylan says.

"Did you try sending it back?" I don't even know if computer games can be sent back when I ask this question. I don't know if he downloaded it, or borrowed it, or even wrote the game himself over summer vacation.

Dylan explains that he bought the game at a gaming store in a strip mall. The packaging had a phone number to call, and he called it. They told him they were aware of the problem and were going to fix it. They said to give them two hours, and try again to log in. He does not remember who he spoke to.

"I just did homework or whatever for like the next few hours and then tried again. Still wasn't working so I fell asleep," he says.

"This sounds very frustrating," I say. "I'm sorry this happened to you. What happened next?"

"Well, like two days later, I tried again. And the same thing happened. I called, they said they knew there was a problem, they were working on it, and nothing got fixed," Dylan says. "I've been stuck playing *Polybius* and *Sad Satan* ever since."

"Okay, I'm going to tell you how to fix this problem, but it's going to require some work from you," I tell the class. "When someone says they are going to fix something in two hours, you need to write their names down, check the game in two hours, and if it's not working, call back."

Your second call would look something like this: "Hi, this

is Dylan. I called at about 10:15 p.m. and spoke to BlueMarine. I told her that the screen was freezing when I tried to log in. She said it would be fixed in two hours. It's close to 12:30 a.m. now, and it's not fixed."

Dylan is looking to log in to *Downward Spiral: Horus Station*. He has notified the company of the problem. Now, he has to follow up and be persistent. The key to fixing this is to *stay on them*. And, if possible, do so without being annoying. This company has a phone number that it gives out with customer service people on the other end. This leads me to believe that they are getting a decent volume of calls with varying degrees of complexity and urgency. Therefore, the problems they are going to solve are the ones they can't get rid of. By checking consistently, and knowing who he spoke to, Dylan has the best chance of getting his problem solved.

This can be a challenge for a university student, especially if they are first-year and getting used to time management. Other responsibilities like family, job, and extracurricular activities can all delay his ability to keep contacting the gaming company. At the same time, though, I'm betting that if he pursues this closely for a day or two, his problem will be solved.

Does it matter that he let it drop and now wants to pick it up again? Not at all. He just has to expect that he will have to start from scratch because he doesn't have a record of when he called or who he spoke to. He has to try to log in again. If it doesn't work, he can call the number and explain his situation. He can mention that it's not his first time contacting them; maybe they have a record of the previous calls.

Let's say BlueMarine from customer service told Dylan that they knew there was a problem and were working on it, but didn't give a time frame. Dylan could have answered, "Oh, great. I'm happy you're working on it. When do you think I'll be able to log in?" or, "I can't wait — what time do you suggest I log back in again?" He then has to make note of the info she gives him and try again when she suggests. If it works, great.

If it doesn't work, Dylan needs to call back, and give a brief history of his situation. It might look like this: "Hi, is this Blue-Marine? I'm not sure if you remember me, it's Dylan. We spoke a few hours ago about the screen freezing? I still am not able to log in. Any news?" Or: "Hi, this is my fourth time calling about the same problem, and I would really like some help." Dylan would then go on to list the days and times of his other calls and who he spoke to and what they said. If none of these calls work, Dylan can ask to speak to a manager or supervisor, let them know what's been happening, and ask for an update. He will need to follow up and check at regular intervals until he gets access to the game.

Dylan also has the option of returning his game to the store. The reason I am not recommending that up front is because Dylan wants to play *Downward Spiral*. The only way he will be able to play is if they let him log in using his name and password. Based on the way I understand the problem, many people are facing the same glitch. If Dylan believed that there was something wrong with his version, then for sure my advice would be to return the game and start again. Because he is being told that this bug is fixable — and being fixed — I am recommending that he follow up as much as possible, as close to the suggested intervals as he can.

When I first set out to give you this example, I was thinking that asking a gamer to be persistent and follow up was counter-intuitive. If I close my eyes and picture someone who spends hours killing imaginary Mario brothers, I think of them as pale and lacking in follow-through, with one hand in a bag of ja-lapeño cheese puffs. But, upon reflection, I have changed my mind. Hours spent following zombies into caves and scorpi-ons into outer space may bring out the more persistent side of a person, and therefore asking a gamer to stay on the soft-ware company is asking him or her to do what they do best. Although, in the end, it doesn't really matter if it comes nat-urally or not — this is what you need to do to get what you want when you are continually promised that something will be fixed "later."

You need to understand what time "later" is so that you can set your alarm for "later," and follow up. Every time you forget to follow up, just know that the clock rolls back a bit, and it may take you a little while to get started again.

When Else to Use This Technique

This technique also works if you are waiting for someone to get back to you with information that you need. For example, the bank. Let's say you go to the bank to purchase a money order, and when you get home, you realize that you were charged twice for the same transaction. You call, and the person tells you it will be corrected by the end of the business day.

It's easy to assume it will be taken care of and not check online to make sure. Or to get caught up in one more episode of *Money Heist* and forget to verify that the charges were re-versed.* But don't give in to that temptation, because if you forget to check, one of three things will happen. One, they will forget to correct the error and you will not get your money

---

*   I haven't actually watched *Money Heist*.

back, and it will slip your mind until three weeks later at which point the history will have been erased from your banking app, and it will be that much more complicated to track down the correct details. Or, second possibility, the bank will forget to correct the error, you will forget about the error, and you will be incorrectly charged until time immemorial. Third scenario — if you're lucky — you'll forget but the bank will remember, and you will think you won a very small lottery until you remember that you had a credit coming to you from the time you were double-charged for a money order. I hate to be cynical, but I think the third scenario is the least likely.

When you have something at stake like a charge that is owed to you, I think it is your responsibility to keep very close track of where it's at. You can ask the bank for specifics about when to expect the charge will be reversed, and just like in the video game log-in example, check back at the appointed time. If you forget, go back a step and start again with a phone call to customer service.

Whether you are waiting for a video game log-in or a bank charge to be reversed, the best way to get what you want is to stay on the company and follow up regularly.

 # How to Get Your Money Back When Your Favorite Dress Is Ruined

Some Questions Remain Unanswered

People call me for complaint advice all the time, and usually I have a clear solution in mind. Once, in a job interview, they asked me if I had a vision for how I would run the organization for the next five years. I answered that I had a vision for how I would like my Diet Pepsi poured. In other words, I have a vision for nearly every move I make, and usually when it comes to advocating for myself, I know exactly what to say and to whom.

But not always.

I speak to my friend Jess on the phone almost every day, and that's not her real name because if I gave it to you, you'd probably call her yourself — she's a great listener, and I'm not willing to share.

Jess just hosted her son's Bar Mitzvah, which was a lovely Saturday night affair with a soccer-themed dance floor and matching candy buffet bar. She wore a beautiful black dress that was partially chiffon-y mesh but in the most tasteful possible way.

The floor is swept and the gifts are opened, and Jess now has to run around doing all her post-Bar errands, including dropping off her dress at the same dry cleaner she has been using for almost a decade. She is concerned about the chiffon-y mesh (which I'm sure is not the technical term, but picture black nylon with a black-dot pattern as sort of a yoke around the neck), and takes her time pointing out the delicate hook-and-eye closure at the back to make sure it will not catch on the fabric.

The dry cleaner is attentive and listens to Jess's instructions.

She comes back a week or two later to pick up the dress, and the mesh is perfect. But the rest of the dress is not. The fabric of the dress has pilled and pulled so that it looks more distressed than the purposely distressed Oriental rugs so popular in New York a few years ago. Jess, too, is now distressed. This is the dress she wore to her son's Bar Mitzvah. It has sentimental value, not to mention real-world value. She bought it at a small store on a small street where everything is tiny, except, of course, the price tags. I should mention that Jess is professionally fit and could fit in my pocket.

She calls her mother, who suggests that she bring the dress back to the little store where she bought it and show them the damage.

"I have the same dress," says the salesperson, "and I have not had any problem with it. The fabric on my dress is fine."

I wasn't there, but I'm picturing the salesperson as one of those pencil-skirted bosses from the movies with a slicked-back bun who starts wearing her hair down once her personality loosens up.

"Have you dry-cleaned the dress?" Jess asks.

"I have not," says the salesperson, skirt tight, white blouse tucked in.

Until she cleaned the dress, Jess had not had a problem either. There is no way to point this out without being rude. Jess shows her the tag on the dress. "I followed the directions exactly. It says Dry Clean Only, and I brought it to the dry cleaner. Is it normal for the fabric to pill like this?"

"It is not normal. The fabric is very sensitive. Are you sure you didn't sit on anything abrasive? Emery boards? Concrete tile?"

"Yes, I am sure," Jess says. "I bought the dress, I wore it to my son's Bar Mitzvah, and I didn't sit down all night! I brought it to the cleaners, as suggested, and when I picked it up, this is how it looked!"

Salesperson says nothing.

"Would it be possible for you to check and see if this dress is still available in this color and size?" Jess asks.

Ideally, she would like to have the dress replaced by the store. The salesperson is not being super helpful. When I imagine this scene playing out, I picture her movie hair still pulled into a tight bun. At this point, Jess is gathering information. She would like to know if the replacement option is even available to her, or if she needs to figure out a Plan B.

The salesperson says she doesn't have the dress available, but she will check around for it, which will take a few days.

Jess leaves with the dress and goes back to the dry cleaner. She shows them the damage. They offer to refund her for the cleaning. She says she wants more than that. They say there is really nothing more they can do — when something is made with cheap fabric, it may get damaged. "This fabric is a lot of things, but cheap is not one of them," Jess says, partially out of frustration and partially out of plain honesty.

The owner of the dry-cleaning store comes from the back to tell Jess that because she is such a loyal customer, and because she explained to them how delicate the dress was, he personally cleaned it. He shows her how he protected the hook-and-eye closure with a special foil so that it wouldn't catch on the chiffon-y mesh. He shows her how he hung the dress lovingly and carefully. Jess is not sure what to do. Her mom told her that cleaners usually have insurance to cover mishaps like this one. No one is mentioning insurance.

"What can you do to help me replace the dress?" Jess asks the owner.

He shows her the cleaning ticket and points to the fine print, which states that they are not responsible for any damage or loss. He then offers to take another careful pass at the dress, and see if he can remove some of the pillage without pillaging the integrity of the garment.

Jess feels she has nothing to lose at this point and leaves the dress with him.

The salesperson's assistant calls her from the store a few days later to say that they have found the dress in the same color and size, would Jess like to *purchase* it again, clearly indicating that they have no intention of replacing a dress that has been worn and dry-cleaned, even though it was damaged following directions on the tag.

Jess then goes to pick up the dress from the dry cleaner. She has to admit there is an improvement, but it is definitely not in the shape it was in when she dropped it off. The dry cleaner has waived the fee for cleaning the dress the first time, cleaned it a second time at no charge, and seems genuinely concerned that Jess be satisfied with the outcome of this situation.

Jess asks me what I think she should do, and I'm really not sure. This is a case where my vision abilities are on the fritz. On the one hand, the dry cleaner must have done something to the dress to make it pill like that. To me, the fact that they were able to sort of fix it is incriminating, because that could mean that they were the ones who futzed with it in the first place. On the other hand, they were at least willing to help. They also have a ticket that clears them of any responsibility, yet they still refunded the cleaning charge and attempted to mitigate the damage.

The teeny store is selling (miniscule) clothes and advising people about how to care for them. If their instructions wreak havoc on the fabric, there should be recourse, such as a refund or exchange. If they are knowingly selling expensive garments that don't clean properly, then that seems borderline fraudulent to me. If they are not aware of this, and the damage is as much a surprise to them as it is to us, then shouldn't they have a beef with the designer and her (no doubt tiny) atelier?

The only other option I can think of is for Jess to contact the designer directly and let them know what happened to her dress. If they are willing, she could send them copies of all the receipts (store and dry cleaning), along with photos of the damage or even the damaged dress itself, and see if they would be willing to send her a new one.

Some complaints do not have simple resolutions. Sometimes it's just about trying your luck by taking a few different approaches and hoping that someone will replace your dress.

A few things have already gone well here — Jess remained

calm, she had receipts for all her transactions, and she followed up with all the parties. Still, everyone seems to think that.everyone else is responsible for the pilling of the dress. No one is willing to cover the expense of a replacement.

I am sorry that I don't have more to offer you in this case, Jess. I think you can keep trying, and maybe your squeaky wheel will get the grease. In the meantime, though, I'm going to pour myself a Diet Pepsi and see what else I can come up with for you.

I am sharing this story because I want you to understand that, although sometimes there is no direct path to making sure your voice is heard, you still have to speak up. There are no right answers. Well, there might be a few right answers, but most of the time, any speaking up is better than no speaking up at all.

Another Dry Cleaner Story with a Different Ending

When it comes to cleaners, I believe that good customer service really can be a differentiating factor. Years ago, I brought my cleaners a collection of suits and dresses that my family of five needed for an event out of town. They swore up and down to me that it all would be ready Wednesday after work so that I could pack it up in time for our Thursday flight. When I got there, everything was ready except for my son Benji's suit pants, which they couldn't find. Stores were closed, suits were mandatory, and there was no way to solve this problem other than to insist that the dry cleaner scour the premises to find the missing trousers. They turned up in a boiler room where they had been hung to dry, but someone had forgotten to press them. They couldn't press them when I got there because the equipment had been turned off and was too cold to operate. In the end, they said I could stop by at 6:15 a.m. on my way to the airport, and the pants would be ready. I didn't trust them 100 percent, but I felt it was my only option under the circumstances, and guess what? The cab driver was a little surprised when I asked him to stop by the cleaners en route to the airport, but the pants were pressed, we were impressed, and Benji was appropriately dressed.

I am not sure what the same dry cleaner would have done if the suit pants appeared discolored or damaged. They provided outstanding customer service to me, and I have been loyal to them ever since, but Jess's situation appears considerably more complicated.

13 How to Get Your Teacher to Raise Your Grade

Show the Evidence

When I was pregnant with Ezra, and things weren't going so well, I promised myself that if we all pulled through (we did), and the baby that was supposed to be born in April made it to April (he did), then I would have Friday night dinner with my family every week (I do). Over the past twenty years, I have made it a priority to follow the Jewish tradition of sitting down to Friday supper with my family, and my sister's family, and my dad, and whoever else is around.*

For the past few years we've had a parade of college students join the gang, and since we are their surrogate parents

---

* Admittedly, last Friday I took Liberty to see *Disney on Ice*, but that was more the exception than the rule.

(at least for the evening), we sometimes have the opportunity to dispense advice.*

Please join me at my sister's house on a Friday night. One of the kids — let's call him Jethro the Fine Arts Student — is sitting with his head in his hands. To qualify for an internship at the museum, Jethro had to get at least a C+ in the Renaissance to Rococo survey course. Things didn't go as planned. "He failed me," Jethro says, "and now I can't even apply for the internship."

First of all, comments like "he failed me" are not going to win me over. If you fail a course, I need you to admit at least partial responsibility. Saying that someone else failed you makes it sound like it was arbitrary. You are suggesting that all the students sat in the class, submitted assignments, completed exams, and then were subjected to an academic lottery where the professor picked out who he would pass and who he would fail. I doubt it happened that way. I don't mind if you tell me you believe you were graded unfairly, or graded too harshly, but I need you to accept at least partial responsibility for your grade.

"Do you know your professor?" I ask. "Does he or she know you want the internship? Have you tried talking to them? Is your class huge? What was the grade breakdown?" My kids often complain that I ask way too many questions, and in retelling this story, I see they have a point.

Jethro explains that they were graded based on a midterm, a final, and two homework assignments, with 10 percent for

---

*   My friends and family members have been sending their kids to college in Montreal, and we've been so happy to have them join us for dinner.

participation. He says that it was a large class, that he sort of knows the professor, and that he has tried talking to him.

"I went to his office hours today," Jethro says. "I told him I needed six extra points on the final exam to move my F to a C+ and then I'd be out of his hair. He barely looked up from his computer."

Oy, Jethro. Too bad you couldn't come to Friday night dinner last week. I would have preferred to give you some advice before you spoke to the prof. But — all is not lost. "Jethro, I'm not sure if this is fixable, but I have an idea or two that might work," I say.

I explain to Jethro that the distribution of grades in a class has to follow the course outline, also known as the syllabus. That is considered the student-faculty contract. If the course outline states that your grade is 30 percent midterm, 50 percent final, 5 percent each homework assignment, and 10 percent participation, then everyone in the class has to be graded using the same breakdown. The grades on each of these assignments have to add up to the final grade. Therefore, the professor can't give you six or eight or fourteen extra points just because you need them. You, the student, have to find the missing marks, and point out to the professor where — in which assignment or exam — you might be able to find some points to boost your overall score.

I suggest to Jethro that he ask to see his exams (and any other assignments that may not have been returned to him). He may spot a calculation error or an answer that the grader missed that might be able to improve his mark quickly. If he sees anything like that, I suggest he politely point it out to the professor, in person if possible. He might say something like "Excuse me, I have a question. Do you see here where the multiple-choice questions add up to 30? I got them all right, but for some reason mine only add up to 23. Am I missing something?" The professor will then either say, "Oh, you're right. I'm sorry," and hand him the missing 7 points on a silver platter. Or he will say, "That's because I had to deduct 7 points for your wrong answers over here," and show him where he lost points. If he has a conflict regarding how the exam was graded, then I suggest he check his school's regulations. Many colleges have academic reevaluation procedures designed for when an unresolvable discrepancy occurs.

Another thing Jethro can try is the participation grade. He can ask the professor what grade he received for participation, and how it was calculated. If he wasn't awarded the full 10 percent, he may be able to convince the professor to bump him up in this area because of the great questions he asked or because of his consistent attendance in class.

The other option Jethro has is to ask for a supplemental exam or assignment. Sometimes professors will let a student retake the final in an effort to boost their grade. This may mean waiting until the course is offered again another semester, and delaying the internship, and Jethro will have to think about whether he wants to do that. If he is willing to delay his internship application until next year, his school may offer him this option, and have his new grade replace the old one.

A few weeks later, it's my turn to host dinner, and Jethro shows up. "I did what you said, and I am happy to report there was a calculation error in my midterm," he says.

"Bruh,"* says one of the other student dinner guests.

"Right? I pointed it out to the professor, and he had no

---

*   Slang for "You're kidding."

choice but to give me the marks once I showed him where they were," Jethro says.

I'm happy that things worked out for our student dinner guest. What I want you to learn from this example is that if your grades fall short of what you need — for admission to another program, for an award, or for an internship, you may be able to get them raised, but it will be up to you to figure out where the missing points will come from. It is important to present the professor with the evidence that he or she needs to assist you.

When Else to Use This Technique

You can use this technique when asking for a discount in an informal retail scenario. Let's say you're at a craft fair, and you really want the yellow beaded earrings because they remind you of sunshine, and it's been a long, gray winter. However, the earrings are $45, way more than you think they're worth. If you would like to pay less than the indicated price, you will have to give the seller a reason.

There are two steps to this process. First, make a connection with the seller before you jump into the ask. Suggested conversation openers:

- "Oh, I love these earrings. Did you make them yourself?"
- "Aren't you just craving color this time of year? These earrings are adorable!"
- "I like all your work, but these yellow ones are spectacular."

Next, look at the earrings closely to see if there is any justification to lower the price. Maybe one of the beads is discolored. Maybe one of the earring posts is bent. Maybe one earring is longer than the other. If there is a flaw, it would be on you to point this out to the seller, to give her a reason to charge you less.

You can say something like "Oh-h. One of these looks a bit shorter than the other. Is it supposed to be like that?" Wait for answer. My guess is that they will say something like "Let me see it?" Then you show what your concern is and say, "Is there any chance we could reduce the price?" or, "Do you think that's sufficient to justify a price reduction?" or, "The $45 price tag seems steep for earrings with a bent post. Would you take $30?"

If there is absolutely nothing wrong with the earrings, but you still want a price reduction, you can try to give other reasons for dropping the price. You might point out another table where comparable earrings are way less expensive or ask about other things at this booth that seem more reasonably priced. If there is nothing else, you can always try this: "I love these earrings, but $45 is way out of my budget. Would you accept $35?" You don't want to go so low as to be insulting, but you can definitely ask to knock a few bucks off.

In both of these scenarios it's up to you to provide the evidence to back up your request. Whether you are looking for an increase in a grade like Jethro or a decrease in the cost of a pair of earrings, you need to offer a reason for people to give you what you want.

14 How to Stay Alive While Your Complaint Is Being Investigated

Remain Calm

Please ignore the space-time continuum and meet me in July 2012, let's call it a Tuesday, at around 11:30 a.m.

I am working as an ombudsperson in a university-affiliated long-term care center. This means it's a nursing home that looks after a frail aging population in the most compassionate possible way. There are outdoor barbecues and intergenerational programming. There are live music concerts and french fries on the menu. It is a publicly funded establishment with the highest standards of care in North America.

I am there to make sure that everyone is treated fairly. If there are problems with the care being received, the residents or their families can come and see me, and I help straighten everything out. I see a variety of cases, ranging from people who don't like the artwork in the hallway to those who feel they are being handled too roughly. There is an overall openness to correcting any issues. In this environment, the ombudsperson is a government-mandated position. Every health-care institution in the province of Quebec* must have a "Complaints Commissioner," or ombudsperson. I am there one or two days a week, and I have an open-door policy.

My office is on the main floor, next to the fundraising department and across the hall from the cafeteria. One day, a tall man with blue eyes and white hair comes to see me. His name is Mr. Cloutier.† He begins to speak, and I notice that he is getting paler and paler. I offer to go across the hall and get him a paper cup of water. He waits in my office.

I come back and hand him the water, which he sips. Mr. Cloutier continues his story. I am listening, unsure if he's shouting or just being emphatic. "My wife Agnes came in here three years ago because I just couldn't look after her at home anymore. Her mind is fine, but she wasn't able to DRESS herself or COOK for herself, and it just became TOO much for one person."

"I understand," I say. I am not sure yet what I can do for him, although sometimes clients just need a compassionate ear.

Wife used to walk with a walker, and she would walk from her room upstairs to the elevator and come down to meet him for a coffee. Then that became too difficult for her, and he would go upstairs to meet her, and together they would come down to the lobby. The past couple of weeks have been hard on Agnes. She had a cold, and a flu, and now she's out of bed, but

---

*   A province is like a state, but in Canada. Quebec is the one with the poutine.

†   Not his real name, but the name of our neighbor when I was a little girl and one of the first truly old men that I ever met.

they have offered her the use of a wheelchair, because she really is not able to walk.

"I don't want my Agnes in a wheelchair. The IDEA of it. the THOUGHT of my AGGIE, who used to hustle and watusi with the best of 'em, stuck in a WHEELCHAIR. I mean, who are the ANIMALS who are suggesting this? I would like a FULL INVESTIGATION."

I am rapidly experiencing many emotions.

- I feel terrible for Agnes's husband. Aging is tough; caring for a sick loved one is tough; nursing homes — even the best possible ones — can be tough. Poor guy.
- The love he feels for his wife is beautiful and must be acknowledged.
- Mr. Cloutier is screaming and getting very upset, and he has still not articulated what specifically warrants a full investigation.
- He is pale and getting clammier by the second. I hope to all that is holy that he does not pass out (or worse) in my office.

Sometimes, to calm people down in such situations, I ask them questions that cause them to pause for a moment and reminisce. I ask how he and Agnes met. I am hoping that they met by a cool river on a warm sunny day so that maybe the image of his beloved under a weeping willow or a towering pine will give this gentleman a chance to collect himself.

Bad idea. They met after World War II. Having both lost their families in the war, they were sent to a displaced persons camp in Europe, where, among the disease and the army-issued tents, seventeen-year-old Agnes Rothenburg and sixteen-year-old Napoleon* Cloutier fell in love. There was no one to give permission for them to be married because both of their families had perished, so they lived together illegally until they had both passed their eighteenth birthdays, at which point they found someone who would perform the ceremony. This is a beautiful story of love among the ruins, but it does nothing to calm this gentleman down.

"This WHEELCHAIR idea is [*inhale*] NUTS [*exhale*]. I absolutely will [*gasp*] NOT have AGNES [*inhale*] using ANYTHING of the SORT!" he says.

"Sir." I put my hand on his. "I'm worried about you. You are very upset right now."

"OF COURSE I'm upset. Wouldn't YOU [*gasp*] BE?"

"Yes. I can understand that things are not going your way. I need to call the unit, though, and have a nurse come down. Maybe she will be able to help you."

Complaining and health are closely tied together. Studies have shown that emotions like anxiety can be related to the onset of coronary heart disease (CHD) and that anger is a close second. I am interested in this type of research, but I am not looking to prove this hypothesis right here at my office desk.

Mr. Cloutier reluctantly agrees, and I bring him out to the tables near the cafeteria until my friend Carole, a head nurse from upstairs, comes to take a look at him. I leave the two of them alone and go back to my office. I leave my door open in case they come back or someone else comes by to see me.

A few minutes later, I see two ambulance guys walk by with an empty stretcher. I peek out of my doorway, and I see them lifting Mr. Cloutier up and strapping him into position.

---

* First name of another beloved neighbor from my childhood.

One says to the other, "What the hell happened to this guy? He looks awful."

"He was with the ombudsman," is the response. As if being with the ombudsperson is a medical explanation. A substitute for "His BP is 11/40," or "His creatinine is dropping," or whatever these medical techs normally shout at each other.

I don't want you to end up in the back of an ambulance because you are complaining. I want you to be able to articulate your complaint calmly and rationally, and not become so upset or agitated that someone has to call 911.

I know that some complaints are deeply upsetting, and that some situations warrant being stressed out. However, when you walk into the ombuds office or your manager's office or anywhere else where you are asking for something, you need to get yourself as calm as possible before you walk through the door.

First, when you are calm, you sound more rational, and the other person is more likely to listen to what you have to say. Second, when you are calm, you will remember all the points in your argument, and you will be able to articulate them all. Third, if you are stamping your feet and jumping up and down, it's much easier for the other party to discount you out of the gate and say things like "Crazy lady in Aisle Two complaining that the flowers aren't fresh," instead of taking your complaint seriously and stopping to smell the flowers to determine whether you have a point.

There are all kinds of articles claiming that complaining is not good for your health. They say that your blood pressure goes up, and that negativity leads to depression, which could lead to further negative health outcomes. I would argue that keeping your feelings inside could be detrimental, and that not learning how to ask for what you want could lead you to a life of settling for second or third best, which could lead to depression, which could lead to further negative outcomes.

However, if you are super riled up, you might think you can be articulate, but the truth is that waiting a while can help your cause. Once the initial sting is gone, you might still be upset because you were treated unfairly, but you will no longer feel that your hair is on fire. That would allow you to bring your complaint forward in a calmer fashion. (This doesn't work for everything, like it would be strange to come back to the gym three days later and say the kettlebell was kinda sticky.)

My auntie Havie* used to have a collection of old charms and family jewelry that she called her amulets. She kept them in a little burgundy pouch and would bring them with her to stressful situations. Just knowing that she had some broken costume jewelry in her purse would help her feel calm. Take a few moments to think about what your amulets might be, and consider arming yourself with them next time you have to complain.

Another option is to bring someone with you who makes you feel calm. Sometimes if you are with a friend or partner or family member, you may be grounded enough to bring your concerns forward and ask for what you need. Again, this isn't always appropriate. For example, if you bring your service llama to the dentist to complain that the novocaine wore off too soon, your complaint may not be taken too seriously. I'm relying on you to use basic human judgment.

Let's go back to the original complaint and pull it apart a bit. The gentleman was upset that his beloved wife was offered

---

*   Havie is her family nickname. Her given name is Eleanor.

a wheelchair. He felt she wasn't being given a fair chance at rehabilitation. He could request to see the rehab assessment and/or to meet with the specialist(s) who determined that a wheelchair would be the best choice for her. If he was not satisfied with the assessment provided by the nursing home, he could ask to bring in someone else to give a second opinion (at his expense). I suggest asking before bringing in an external professional for three reasons. First, some nursing homes have policies against outside providers, and will not follow any recommendations that don't come from their own staff. Second, I think relations with the nursing home will be better if he is transparent and says something like "Agnes used to get second opinions on everything from paving the driveway to selecting finials for our curtain rods. I owe it to her to get her a second opinion for her health." Third, the nursing home itself may have experience with contract rehab therapists and might be able to suggest someone.

If it turns out that Agnes's health has indeed deteriorated, and a wheelchair is the best bet to aid her mobility, the staff has a role to play in educating her husband (and Agnes herself, if appropriate) about her condition and what to expect. Healthcare professionals of all education and skill levels often struggle with how to deliver bad news (e.g., "Your health is deteriorating"), but I have learned that knowing what is coming next is better than being surprised, even if the trajectory is tragic. It is possible that part of what is so upsetting to Mr. Cloutier is that he expected Agnes to fully recuperate from her flu and is surprised that her functioning will not return to what it was. If we were to interview the involved staff, they may say that they tried to talk to Mr. Cloutier about it, and he was not willing to listen. This may be true. That's where I would suggest that they be creative in their communication efforts. For example, Mr. C might be the type of person who takes a few days to digest information. Maybe he was overwhelmed by facing the whole multidisciplinary team in one conference room. If the organization can offer it, Mr. C might benefit from several smaller one-on-one meetings where things could be explained slowly, and he could have the chance to ask questions. Or, if Mr. C brings a family member or a friend to the meeting to help him remain calm, as I mentioned, they might also be able to assist him with taking notes and processing information. Finally, he might be the type who processes written better than oral information, in which case he could be given pamphlets to read and/or relevant internet links to check out when he gets home.

A few weeks after Mr. Cloutier was taken away by ambulance, I bumped into him in the garden. I greeted him warmly and told him I was happy to see him outside in the sunshine with his wife. He said I looked familiar but he didn't remember my name. I gently reminded him that I was the ombudsman and that he had been to my office to talk about his wife and her wheelchair. "I'm so sorry," he said. "That was such a stressful time for me, I don't remember a thing about that day. I know I was complaining, but I don't remember any of the details."

His wife sat beside him, in her wheelchair, beaming. She was clearly enjoying the outdoors, which may not have been possible for her without the aid of a wheelchair.

I told him I understood that what seemed like a giant complaint at the time became smaller when he adjusted to his wife's new reality. Also, passing out and being taken to the hospital was frightening, and he didn't want to go down that road again.

Being calm when you ask for what you want has several benefits. You will get your point across more clearly, you will be less likely to suffer adverse health effects, and you will gain clarity about whether you would like to file a formal complaint.

Questions for Reflection

1. Do you believe that stress is bad for your health? What do you think is more stressful: speaking up about something that is bothering you and trying to fix it, or sweeping your problem under the rug, where it is likely to grow and fester, like a giant wound?

2. What would you bring with you to calm your nerves if you had to lodge a complaint with an ombudsman or other official-sounding office? Think about a few objects or photographs that you could set aside to remind you to stay grounded. If possible, put these items together in a pouch or a drawer so that you can grab them quickly if you ever need to.

3. I talked to this gentleman about his past to try and make him feel better. It totally backfired. What would you have done differently (*better* is implied) in this situation? What else could I have talked about that might have been easier on this poor gentleman's heart?

PART II

I Want You to Change

The theme of this book is how to ask for what you want so that you can get what you need, and sometimes what we want is for someone else to change. We believe that if we could just get the other person to fall in line, our lives will be greatly improved. All the issues in this section relate to trying to change other people's behavior. Here are a few examples:

- You want your cubiclemate to start brushing their teeth so that you don't have to smell their smoked paprika herring breath.
- You want your cousin to be on time and stop keeping everyone waiting.
- You want your spouse to put down his or her cellphone and pay attention to what you're saying.

There are a few ways to look at this set of problems.

On the one hand, you can only control yourself and your own behavior. You can't get someone else to quit smoking. You have the right to control your own environment, though, so you can say, "You can't smoke in my house. I would love to see you, but if you need to smoke we should probably meet at *blank*." I say *blank* because I'm having trouble thinking of a place where you can freely smoke in Montreal. And it's way too cold to meet outside today — January 15 — for me to think about park benches or outdoor *terrasses*.* "If you can come up with a place we can meet and you can smoke, then I'm happy to get together with you. I'm not telling you to quit smoking; I'm telling you there is no smoking at my place." You get to control what happens in your home.

The other way to look at it is that some people don't know when their behavior is negatively impacting others, so we may have to gently nudge them in the right direction. Maybe they don't realize their armpits are giving off signals that send cockroaches scurrying back to the carboniferous period.† Maybe they don't realize that they speak too loudly, or too closely, or that they spit when they talk. This section will give you some suggestions for how to correct behavioral changes that are sensitive but could greatly improve your standard of living, or at least, smelling.

Finally, there are situations where we want someone to change, but it turns out we are wrong. We may think someone is being malicious or lethargic or sloppy, but they are just misunderstood. We may not be able to change their behavior, but we may find it within ourselves to become more compassionate and accepting. Our role may be to reframe and reconsider what we think we need in favor of what we can offer all humanity.

---

*   French for outdoor restaurant, bar, or café seating, very popular in summer here.

†   That is, about 320 million years ago.

How to Get
Your Guests to Arrive
on Time for Dinner

Learn the Serenity Prayer

The other day I was invited to speak at a Mom Lunch. That's a lunch where a gaggle of moms get together and drink white wine and eat sushi, and they have guest speakers (such as myself).

I have my eyebrows plucked professionally, buy a new lipstick, and find a parking spot right in front. It's a beautiful sunny day, the perfect backdrop for a conversation about complaining. One of the moms, Annie, gets up to introduce me, and says that she heard me speak a few years ago and that she raised her hand that day and asked a question. The advice I gave her, she says, changed her life. "Ooooh," I say, "tell me more." Humility is something I'm working on.

I'm going to give you the same advice I gave to Annie, and if you are ever introducing me at a talk you can let me know if it worked. Here's a flashback to the original meeting when Annie asked her question.

"I have a complaint, and I need your advice," Annie says. I like her already. She knows what she wants and she's going after it. I can't tell you how many people open with a list of allergies, a family tree, and a regime of prescription medications before they actually get to their question. This one is a heat-seeking missile.

Annie has a close family with lots of cousins and aunts and uncles. They like to get together on Sundays for a traditional spaghetti-and-meatball dinner starting at 5 p.m. The time was established so they can relax and have a drink before they eat, and still get home at a reasonable hour on a work/school night. Because of the size of her dining room, the generosity of her heart, and the quality of her meatballs, Annie hosts 100 percent of the time. Annie's cousin Betty, Betty's husband, and their three kids are always late.

"I have a few questions," I say. "First, how late is she?"

Here's why I need details: While I'm the first to say that feelings are never wrong, and if Annie is unhappy with the lateness then the specifics don't *really* matter, the truth is that I want to know what we're dealing with here. Is Annie overreacting? Is she the type of person who thinks if you aren't fifteen minutes early, you're late? Or is Cousin Betty genuinely, disrespectfully, late to family dinner?

"She's usually always about, um, about forty-five minutes to an hour late. Probably an hour," Annie says.

Yeah, I agree that an hour late is hard to ignore, especially if you're hosting dinner for a bunch of people. Annie has a point.

"My second question is, Have you tried talking to her about this? And if so, what does she say?" I ask. I want to know if Annie has directly confronted Betty. I am wondering if she's asked her point-blank why she can't be on time.

"Yeah, I've tried talking to her about it, for sure. She always has an excuse. Someone lost their house keys, we had to stop and pick up milk on the way, the dog needed to be let out," she says.

Now we have another clue to help us solve this puzzle: The excuses are varied. I was wondering if there was one consistent reason for her lateness — for example, if Betty or her husband worked Sundays and had a shift that finished around 5 p.m., it would be impossible for them to get to Annie's on time. I would say the same thing for a kid's basketball practice or pottery class — anything that would cause automatic, built-in lateness week after week. Had Betty given something like that as her reason, I might have suggested changing the dinner time, even if temporarily, to accommodate her and her crew. However, she is giving a rainbow of reasons, which appear to be based more on lack of internal planning than an external construct like a job or a class.

Here's my final question: "Why is this Betty situation getting to you?"

"Because she knows how much it bothers me that she's late, and she says it won't happen again. Then the next week we're back to the same story," Annie says. "I want to know how to complain effectively about this. What can I say to her that will cause her to just show up on time?"

"What have you tried?" I ask.

"I've bought her a countdown timer she can wear around her neck. I've had a custom key rack made for her front hall, with everyone's names on it. I've suggested dog walkers. I've installed a time-wasting app on her phone."

"Well, Annie, it sounds like you have been a fantastic cousin to Betty. I have bad news and good news. The bad news is that if there was a way to make this work, I think you would have found it by now. There is nothing I can say to make Betty arrive on time. The good news is that you are in charge of your own behavior, and no one can say anything to change you without your consent."

Annie wants to know what that means in terms of her Sunday night dinner. I explain that her best bet is to send a group text or email to everyone who is invited, including Betty and her group. The email should say that Annie is hosting Sunday dinner this week, and she's really looking forward to seeing everyone. She needs to explain that the dinner is starting at 5 p.m., and they will be sitting down to eat at 5:15 p.m. I advise her to be clear: "Anyone who comes after that is more than welcome to join. You may miss the appetizers, but there will be plenty of pasta to go around!" or something equally cheerful that spells out the plan for the evening.

"What if they get insulted?" Annie asks.

I have two conflicting answers to that. First, we are going to word it in a way that makes it as uninsulting and as gentle as possible. It is certainly not my intention nor your intention to insult anyone. However, and here's the other side of the coin, sometimes you may have to slight someone very slightly to make sure that you get what you want. Annie can't be completely flexible and accommodating to all Betty's whims *and* make sure her dinner starts on the dot at 5 p.m. When both things can't be true, we need to pick between ourselves and the other person, and I'm here to tell you that it's okay to pick yourself.

Annie will get what she needs by reframing what she wants. She is recognizing that, as the dinner host, she is entitled to set the start time and the parameters for the meal. If she still wants to include Cousin Betty, she can, but it doesn't mean that dinner has to be cold, delayed, or congealed on people's plates while they wait for the grand entrance of the Betty contingent. Annie recognizes that by being late, Betty is choosing her needs ahead of Annie's, and so by starting dinner when she wants to, Annie is choosing to put herself first.

When you are complaining effectively, you might begin by confronting the person directly about their behavior, as Annie did with her cousin. If you don't see an improvement, then it's up to you to decide what you want to do next. If someone is doing something harmful or self-destructive and can't stop, more drastic measures (like an intervention) might be called for. But if it's something relatively benign, like lateness, Annie has to prioritize. She can put her need for a 5 p.m. dinner over her inner need to accommodate Betty's chronic lateness.

That's the advice I gave Annie. She told me that ever since then she has sent out an email every time she hosts, telling everyone how happy she is to see them and letting them know that supper is at five. She says it's been working like a charm.

Does this mean Betty has been on time? No, of course not. She has to find her keys and let out the dog and hope that her dog hasn't eaten the keys. Why is Annie less aggravated now? Her dinner starts when she wants it to, and the spaghetti is never overcooked.

The main lesson here is that you can ask for what you want (Betty to be on time) and still not get it because you don't control Betty's behavior. The temptation is to offer her suggestions for improvement like "Hang your keys on a hook by the door" or "Install a doggy door." I am here to tell you that those suggestions will only set you up for disappointment. Betty will not follow your instructions. Or if she does, her keys will fall through the doggy door and present her with another reason to be late. I'm suggesting you can take a step back and realize that what you really want is your dinner to be on time, and that is something you can control.

Reflection

The Serenity Prayer, a cornerstone of twelve-step programs and affirmation-oriented greeting cards, is helpful in reminding us to accept that some things are not changeable. We cannot change Betty's chronic lateness. But some things can be changed, such as what time we sit down to a meatball dinner. And wisdom — well, I'm still working on that one.

Serenity Prayer

God, grant me the serenity
To accept the things I cannot change;
Courage to change the things I can;
And wisdom to know the difference.

16

How to Ask Your Husband to Put Down His Cellphone During Dinner*

Set the Bar Low

Last fall, I was invited to speak to a group of women leaders in philanthropy. These are women who chair committees, balls, and triathlon events to raise money for the needy, such as underprivileged children or the Senkaku mole.† They own helicopters and private jets, and everyone's nails are impeccable. The women, not the moles.

The luncheon is in a private home. Platters are set out across a pink linen tablecloth, and champagne chills on the sideboard.

---

* This story was brought forward by a woman (wife) about her male partner (husband). Please feel free to extrapolate this to anyone who plays this (or any similar) role in your constellation. This is not intended to be heteronormative, or a judgment of any kind, but rather to reflect an actual story, and how it was brought to my attention.

† The Senkaku mole is an endangered species, found on the small Japanese island of Uotsuri-jima.

As people enter and help themselves to crudités, I begin to feel insecure about my speech. First of all, what could this stunning collection of women possibly have to complain about, and second of all, why would they want to take tips from me?

As I nurse a San Pellegrino (soda water but with smaller, more dignified bubbles), and attempt to mingle, everyone is super friendly and acts interested. A few even say they can't wait for my advice. I am sweating in terror but delicately. The upscale vibe is contagious. I need a plan.

I go into the kitchen to collect myself, and next to the sleek iMac computer I spot a stack of index cards and a silver cup filled with perfectly arranged Sharpies set up for me to use in this workshop. This is going to be fun.

The buffet of salads and grilled Pacific bluefin tuna is opened, and everyone helps themselves and takes a seat outside on the cedar deck. I am introduced.

"Welcome, and thank you so much for having me," I say. "We are going to pass around index cards, and I'm going to ask each one of you to write down a problem you would like advice about. This could be a situation where you would like to stick up for yourself but don't have the right words, or a difficult conversation that you have been avoiding."

The women take their time composing their cards. I imagine problems with caterers that serve organic lamb instead of free-range bison, or hairdressers who put caramel streaks on honey blonde instead of honey caramel streaks on natural blonde.

However.

Once again I have indulged in the bad habit of judging books by their glamorous covers. The concerns are varied, and I have a chance to speak to several of them. For example:

- How do you tell your in-laws you don't like the way they are disciplining your child?
- How do you deal with a know-it-all?
- How do you tell a colleague that her expense reports are always filed incorrectly?

I offer some suggestions for each of these, and then I get to the card that I would like to discuss with you today. It says: "How do you get your husband to stay off his cellphone during dinner?"

Huh. Interesting for a bunch of reasons. First, even these women fight the screen war. Screens are a major problem in *everyone's* life, whether you have the latest in technology or a previously loved smartphone that you bought off Craigslist. Second, I would think that their kids would be the worst offenders, not other adults. Third, because I *cannot* tolerate screens at the table, this cause is close to my heart. Finally, I am interested to hear what is going to come out of my mouth because I feel very much out of my depth here, and this is exactly the kind of situation I feared would arise while I was hyperventilating in the kitchen earlier.

I read out the card, and a platinum-blonde ponytail wearing a lime cashmere pullover admits that it's her issue. She explains that she has two children, and they sit down to eat as a family most nights, after hockey practice. (We live in Canada; hockey is a given.) Her husband taps at his phone from the minute he sits down to the minute his plate is cleared by one of the house staff.

She says when she asks him to put down the phone, he says okay, but then doesn't do it. This causes the kids to bring all their devices to the table too, and between *Fortnite* and *House*

Party this family doesn't have a chance to squabble over the roast chicken like everyone else.

I ask her why they all bring phones to the dinner table in the first place.

"My husband runs a business," she explains. "He says he has to be accessible just in case. And the kids say if it's okay for Dad, then it's okay for us."

"Is it a helicopter ambulance business? Organ donation software? An escaped-prisoner alarm system?" I ask, hoping it's something life-threatening.

"No. Nope. And no, but that would be a good one," she says. "He's in real estate."

Judging from the cut of her cashmere, he is not selling darling 1,700-square-foot bungalows on .25-acre wooded lots. I think we are talking full-scale steel-and-glass high-rises in major metropolitan areas. Still, those deals are not taking place during dinner. Or if they are, they can wait fifteen minutes. Or if they can't, if they are so urgent that fifteen minutes can be a deal breaker, then deals like that are not happening every night.

Cashmere has spoken her mind, and she is not being heard. Her husband is insisting on being on his phone even when she has asked him not to.

We can speculate about his motives. Maybe he is compulsively checking his email because he wants to review the loan terms before the vendor gets to it, or the purchase agreement before the bank sees it,* or anything else that could actually pertain to a real estate transaction of gargantuan magnitude. Maybe he is texting his bookie. Maybe he is trying to acquire

---

* I know this makes no sense. The offer to buy is sent to the seller, not to the bank. Please allow for poetic license.

more FarmCash so he can get to Level 27. Here's the thing: For right now, his motives don't matter. What matters is that we are at an impasse.

When we want one thing, and the other person wants the complete opposite, sometimes it seems like there is no way to work it out. We have several tools for this kind of situation. Today, I suggest choosing a manageable goal, something you can both agree on, even if it's less than what you originally wanted.

"How many nights a week do you have dinner together?" I ask.

"Probably four or five."

"And how long does dinner last?"

"At my house, it's about ten minutes," says a petite brunette chin bob, "if we're being real."

"Yeah, ten, maybe twenty," says Cashmere.

"In that case, let's ask your husband which two nights he's willing to designate as device-free, with the understanding that on the other nights he will be able to have his phone and tap away without judgment or recrimination."

"Hey!" says the woman on Cashmere's left, possibly her sister. "Then she's not getting what she wants."

"Well, she's not getting what she wants at all now. In my scenario, at least she's getting what she wants two nights a week."

"What if he won't agree to two nights a week?" someone asks from the back.

"In that case we ask for one night. And if he won't do one night, we ask for minutes. Ten minutes? Five minutes?" I see people nodding.

I explain that once we have an agreement, we have to stick to our end of the deal, not bring up phones or complain on the other days. The hope is that her husband will realize that five, ten, or thirty minutes a week is a small price to pay for not being nagged, er, reminded every single night. The other hope is that Cashmere will have more leverage with her children when at least two nights a week are designated as phone-free.

People seem to like this solution, and tap notes into their, uh, phones. While I agree 100 percent that phones at the table can be very frustrating, there are times — like when people are posting quotes about what I am saying — that I can be persuaded to make an exception.

Questions for Reflection

1. Is screentime a major issue in your life? How have you dealt with it? Is my suggestion something you would try? Why or why not?

2. Are you reading this book on your phone as we speak? Are you the screen offender in the family? What would putting your phone away mean to you? What would be the possible risks? The rewards?

3. Think about a situation where you are at a stalemate. It might be with your spouse, kid, parent, friend, second cousin once removed, or even with yourself. Imagine you have a magic wand. What would you do to move the conflict toward resolution? Now, imagine your magic wand has run out of sparkle dust. What you can live with? What compromise can you sell to the other side? And who will vacuum all the sparkle dust off the carpet?

17 How to Get Your Boss to Stop Changing Her Mind

Report Her to the Fashion Police

I am at a friend's house, and she has other friends over, and we are sitting in the living room chatting about how everyone hates their job. People are talking about quitting, or going out on their own, or buying an alpaca farm. Just kidding, these are not knitters. If there were knitters on the premises, I can guarantee you that raising alpacas would have been a serious part of the conversation.

"I guarantee that I have it the worst," says Catherine.

"Tell us everything," says Ronna, putting her pink Crocs up on the coffee table.

"My boss keeps changing her mind. First, she tells us to wear blue to work. Then she tells us to wear red to work. Then she says, no red, just blue. Then she says, no blue, just red."

"Yeah, that does sound kind of insane. Where do you work?" I ask.

"I'm a receptionist at a hair salon," Catherine says, and as soon as it's out of her mouth, I realize there would have been no other possible response. Her silky black hair falls straight down to her shoulders. Her eyeliner has not run, and her matte red lipstick is flawless. She looks exactly like a receptionist standing behind a long white marble counter at an upscale hair salon. The only other plausible answer she could have given was receptionist at a fashion magazine.

"What's up with your boss?" Ronna asks. Ronna is a veterinary technician. She is wearing scrubs and petting a cat. I like when people remain in character.

Catherine is not happy. "The boss likes us to be color coordinated. Which is fine, but she seems to have trouble selecting the color!!"

"Amy will give you some advice. She does this kind of thing for a living," Ronna says.

Thanks. This party is getting more fun by the minute.

Let me see what I can come up with, because this is a tough one. On the one hand, I can see the boss wanting her staff to present a united look, especially given the nature of her business. On the other hand, I think it makes things difficult for the employees if the look is constantly changing.

"What do you want to happen?" I ask Catherine. "Like, how could this get resolved so that you would be happy?"

"I want her to change. I want to go back to the old boss, where we could wear whatever we wanted to work!" Catherine says.

I explain to her that that may not be possible. I am not sure what's in the boss's mind with this color scheme enforcement, and I don't know that we will be able to get her to see things our way. "Other than getting her to change, what else could you live with?"

"I want to have an organized schedule. I would like to know which days I wear which color," she says.

She has tried talking to her boss about it, but the boss is not willing to budge. She doesn't recognize that she is inconveniencing her staff. As the story spills out of Catherine, we learn that the boss has sent employees home, without pay, because their blue was too powdery or their red wasn't sufficiently rosy. "She has asked people to bring two or three outfits to work so that she can choose what they wear," Catherine says. "She has asked pregnant employees to work behind the desk because she finds the bump 'unseemly.' She has asked men to grow beards one day, shave the next day, and then grow the beard back because she changed her mind."

When Catherine first started talking about a boss who changed her mind, I was imagining someone who says, "Please make twenty copies of this document. Oh, actually I need thirty copies." I was not expecting an attempt to control what people are wearing and how they look in such detail. I think Catherine did the right thing by attempting to talk to her boss, although I don't know exactly what she said.

Catherine has a few choices. First, if she really likes the job, and this is the only major issue, then I suggest that she try to speak to the boss about the color coordinating one more time. She can wait till the next time there's a color change, and then she can say, "I know you want us to all look, like, amazing or whatever, at work, but I feel like you keep changing your mind about the color of the day. It would really help me be organized if we could put together a schedule. Do you mind if I just draft something, and then you can take a look at it?" If the boss says sure, great, then Catherine can put together a sample calendar, and get approval before she passes it around to the rest of the staff. If the boss says no, then Catherine has to think of other avenues to resolution.

The second thing she might do is speak to the other employees to see if everyone agrees. If the staff is all on the same page, this might be a good topic to bring up at their regular staff meeting, and have everyone chime in. That might look like "Boss, I have something I'd like to add to the agenda. Can we please talk about the dress code?" And then once the agenda item came up, I might show photos of other hair salons and how they organize their dress code. Or I might ask the other staff to give examples of when the current policy was carried too far and caused them stress. This may be enough to get the boss to see that greater structure is called for. I suggest to Catherine that this conversation is best in person rather than sending a petition or a group text. I don't want the boss to feel attacked, but I do want her to take this seriously.

If these two ideas don't work, Catherine should find out if the boss has a boss. If she does, then Catherine can go to that person, and let them know that the staff is not unhappy with the color scheme but rather with how it's being executed. Catherine can bring specific examples with dates and times of when she was asked to change her clothes, and when she was sent home without pay because her blue shoes were not sufficiently blue. The boss's boss may be willing to intervene.

There is one final thing nagging at the back of my mind. I'm not sure if the boss has the legal right to dictate what people wear, and I'm not sure if she can suspend her staff without pay for infractions that are based on clothing rules that only she understands. "Catherine, if you can't get through to your boss, you may have to speak to a professional to find out what your rights are. Maybe someone with human resources experience, or maybe the Better Business Bureau," I tell her.

Depending on where Catherine lives, and whether she's unionized or not, and what the regulations for employee protection are, she may have options for recourse. Or, then again, she can always report her boss to the fashion police. Just kidding, there is no such thing. But if there was, I feel like Catherine could make a pretty decent case against forcing a group of grown adults to cultivate a wardrobe of primary colors.

Similar but Not Identical

Let's say you were also at my friend's house the other night, and you listened to everyone moaning about their jobs, and you decided that was all the encouragement you needed to strike out on your own. You are following what has always been a secret dream — you are now a professional photo organizer. People give you their photographs — printed or digital — and you organize them according to client need. You make albums, or memory books, or box the photos up by year and remove duplicates. You charge by the hour.

Part of your job includes going to people's houses and sitting with them as they sift through their photos and decide which project they want to work on first. Your time is valuable.

Here's the problem: One of your clients is constantly changing her mind about when she wants an appointment. She cancels last minute, attempts to reschedule multiple times, and when you do get to her house, she often keeps you waiting for twenty or thirty minutes. She expects to be charged only for the time you actually spend together.

Remember what Maya Angelou said: "When people show you who they are, believe them the first time." If you have a client who cancels once, this could happen to anyone. When she cancels the second, third, and seventeenth time, she is showing a pattern. She is a canceler. And you have a choice to make, as follows:

- You can continue to do business with her and charge her extra in your hourly rate to offset the inconvenience.
- You can continue to do business with her and let her know you will charge for missed/canceled/late appointments.
- You can stop doing business with her.

If you decide to stop doing business with her due to her unreliability, I suggest you finish the project you are currently working on first, if possible. Then, the next time she calls, you can tell her or not. That's up to you. You can say, "I'm sorry I can't work on this next project with you. I know your schedule is unpredictable, and you often need to change our meeting time, but unfortunately, I need to plan my week, so I can't be that flexible." Or you can just say, "Thank you so much for thinking of me. Unfortunately, I'm not taking on new projects at the moment."

If you are starting out your business, or your financial situation is such that every contract is important and you need to make it work, and if charging more isn't feasible for you right now, then you need to find a way to cope with this client's rescheduling that will not drive you crazy. You can bring extra work to do while you're waiting for her, you can convince yourself that this contract is a stepping-stone to greater work, and you can ask her to introduce you to some of her friends or contacts so that she helps you build a network.

When the boss keeps changing her mind, you have some leverage to work with her, and create an improved working atmosphere for everyone. When you are working on short-term photo-related projects, you have less at stake, and it's easier to potentially walk away or to tolerate behavior that is suboptimal. In both cases, you want the person to change, and that's not going to happen, so the work is about how you react to their behavior rather than how you attempt to change it.

18

How to Ask Someone to Freshen Their Breath

Be Direct

My husband, Dave, and I are on the plane on the way back from Julie's wedding in Plantation, Florida.* Dave has been trying to buy a business for about eight months. When the quest started, we thought it was like buying a house. You look around for a while, and then choose something. Maybe you won't have a powder room on the main floor, but the backyard is the size of a football field. Or maybe the kitchen is falling apart, but you're less than a mile from the train. In other words, you expect to compromise. But after eight months of looking for a small business to buy, we have learned that it's more like finding a spouse. You can look forever and not find the right match.

---

* This is the same Julie who whisper-ordered the fries that never came at the beginning of this book. As you can see, the french fry incident didn't impact our friendship.

"I don't think we are going to be able to find a business to buy," I say to Dave, "so maybe we should just start something."

Six months later, Dave is selling and leasing dishwashers to restaurants, hotels, and other large-scale foodservice establishments. He likes the business because it is service oriented. There are technicians on the road visiting clients every single day to make sure all the equipment runs smoothly and everyone is happy.

The problem is that one of the technicians smells. He has the kind of bad breath that makes you wonder if a skunk crawled between his gums and is slowly decomposing. Each exhale threatens to ignite the hair of the person closest to him.

"I've tried offering him mints," Dave says, "but he doesn't like them."

"Have you tried cinnamon? My coach only chews cinnamon gum," offers our daughter Liberty. "I chewed cinnamon gum before tryouts to get on his good side."

"That was smart," says Benji, our middle son.

"Maybe give him a toothbrush? Or disposable breath strips? You can get them off Amazon," suggests Ezra, the oldest.

"I tried all of that. He didn't, er, bite," Dave says.

When someone has bad breath, our first reaction is to give them a toothbrush, toothpaste, dental floss, cinnamon gum, mints, mouthwash, or all of the above. Very often this doesn't work. Possibly the person is not in tune with oral hygiene, because if they were, we would not be in this mess. Possibly the person thinks their routine (maybe brushing with baking soda or pine cones or some other natural remedy that does not include over-the-counter mouthwash) is working, so they have no need for anything else. Possibly they suffer from sinus issues and have a limited sense of smell. Or they have one of those weird diseases that you see on TV where they eat kitty litter or rusted ball bearings. Who knows.

The best way to complain effectively about bad breath is to tell the person directly and offer them ways to address the situation. I'm going to show you exactly how to do that. But first, I need you to ask yourself two questions.

First: Is this bad breath my business? Let's say the person with bad breath is the courier guy at work. You don't see him often, but when you do, you wish you had a gas mask. You have been known to tell him through the intercom, "Just leave the package at the front," even if that means you have to lug twenty pounds of copy paper to the warehouse. He doesn't work for your company, you are not dating him, he is not a blood relative. Therefore, his bad breath is not your business, and I would not suggest confronting him. If there is a courier client satisfaction survey (preferably anonymous), and you are asked about the delivery guy, I could imagine writing something like "His breath is terrible" or "Please ask him to use breath mints," so that his company can deal with this issue directly.

Dave's technician's breath is my business because he is visiting customers and representing the company, and if he smells bad it's like we all smell bad. This is further compounded by the fact that we are selling sanitation, so good hygiene is part of our brand. I want him to change so that he will make a better impression on our customers, and Dave will sell more soap, and then maybe we will eventually be able to go on safari in Africa, which is very much at the top of my bucket list. In other words, this guy's bad breath may be getting in the way of my ability to take a selfie with a real zebra. I must address it.

The second question I would like us all to ask ourselves is this: How much money are we willing to put behind this project? As part of our complaining effectively about the bad breath, we are going to be offering suggestions, and we need to be aware of how far we're willing to go on this thing. Will we support the purchase of an electric toothbrush? A professional cleaning? A hygienist who comes to the house? In such situations, set your limits so that you will not be transported away on a wave of Good Samaritanship when you have this conversation. For the service technician, Dave feels that it's so hard to find the right fit employee-wise, he would be willing to put some money behind cleaning up this guy's act.

Now. Someone needs to have this difficult conversation and tell the technician that his breath smells. I volunteer to come to the office. "I need to talk to you for a minute, please," I say, and lead him to an empty office. "Is it okay if I close the door?" I ask, taking a large inhale of the fresh hallway air.

"Sure," he says. "What's up?"

I ask him some warm-up questions about how he likes working here, and how the customers are. He answers, and we blah blah blah around for a few minutes.

Then I look him straight in the eye, and I say, "We've been having complaints that your breath is not fresh. I am sitting here across from you, and I have to say, I agree."

I let it sink in.

He looks surprised and kind of hurt.

I continue.

"We need you, and all our employees, to smell fantastic when you go out on the road and represent the company. I'm sure you understand."

He nods in agreement, likely afraid to open his mouth at this point, which may be a good thing.

"I think you need to start by seeing a dentist and making

sure that nothing is really wrong. I looked at the company plan, and you do have some dental coverage. After that, you may need to keep some stuff in your car, maybe a toothbrush and some toothpaste? And brush a couple of times a day. Are you okay with that?"

He is okay with that.

If he had said no, then I would go back to Dave and let him know that this employee is not willing to change his habits, and that maybe his suitability as a technician should be questioned. Dave would probably then find out what the laws are about this, because his company is too small to have a human resources (HR) department. If you work someplace with an HR professional, you can seek this advice internally.

Now let's try another scenario. Let's say I sit down with the technician, I tell him that his breath doesn't smell fresh, and his feelings are hurt. Instead of admitting that I've touched a sore spot, he makes things personal. In this version, he says, "Tell me exactly who said what about my breath. I need to know."

The first thing I do is wait a minute and think about how to answer. I don't want to get caught up in an argument with this employee. I don't want to react, jump, or be impulsive. My instinct might be to reply indignantly, "You know I can't tell you who reported you! There are HIPAA regulations!* Oaths of silence! Attorney-client privilege!"† This might turn into him pointing out that I am neither a doctor nor a lawyer and that these rules don't apply. He might ask to waive these rights.

---

* HIPAA is the acronym for an American law for health-care professionals to prevent sharing of personal information and protect privacy. Does not apply to this situation — it's a joke.

† Attorney-client privilege refers to confidentiality regulations for lawyers and clients. Also does not apply to this situation — another joke.

He may ask what HIPAA means because we live in Canada and have different laws. At that point, we may pull out our phones to see what HIPAA stands for, and if it really has one P and two As, and we will be so far from bad breath that it will be difficult to get the conversation back on track.

I want to avoid a distracting argument.

If the technician says something unexpected, my first move will be to pause. I will think about what I want to say next, before I answer.

I may calmly respond, "I understand. I'm sure this is a surprise. You know I can't tell you who said what. And that's not important. What's important is that we've discussed this, and you're going to fix it."

Please note that when I give you suggestions of what to say, I am imagining that you are going to take my words and make them your own. Maybe your voice sounds more like "I see your aura softening as you digest the words I have spoken. Please accept the offerings of our spirit, and know that the specifics of who said what to whom are less important than the collective gift of consciousness that has been provided to you on this day. The greatest act of recognition you can provide is to step forth and take care of your mouth. Let the breath be your guide." Or maybe you're a person of fewer words: "Dude. Your breath. Srsly."

Let's say the technician won't let up. He demands to know what proof I have, who told on him, whether I would like to see the results of his last salivary incubation test.[*] Maybe he feels discriminated against, and says I am picking on him because he is too short, tall, white, black, brown, pale, or freckled. He

---

[*]   Which measures halitosis.

says he's going to call Dave because this is a violation. He is belligerent and defensive.

"My breath is fine! There's nothing wrong with my breath! This is none of your business! Who do you think you are?" and more off-color language and swearing after that.

In that case, I would give him a few minutes to collect himself and then end the conversation. I would drop the subject for a few days, and then come by for a follow-up meeting in which I would ask, "Have you had a chance to think about what we talked about last week? Are you willing to have a conversation about it now?"

If he says yes, we call the dentist and book his first appointment. If he says no, we circle back to Dave and a possible HR consultation.

As I said at the beginning of this story, when you are looking for a business to buy it's kind of like looking for a spouse. You may be worried about pleasing your customers, keeping up with your loan payments, and updating your Snapchat filter, but your biggest problem might just be bad breath. While it may be tempting to breathe downwind or install an aromatherapy diffuser, your best chance at success is to address the problem as directly as possible.

It Happened to Me

I am on the way home from work, and I call my sister-in-law Nicki to catch up. She asks me about this book and how it's progressing. Specifically, she wants me to give her an example of what kind of problems people in the book have and what kind of advice I am giving them.

"There's a chapter on what to do if someone has bad breath," I say, "and—"

She jumps in, "Oh, so you told them about the time that I—"

"Uh, no, I didn't mention my own—"

"I think you should," Nicki declares. If she ever decided to sell luxury cars, Lexus would have to build a new plant to keep up with the increased demand. In other words, Nicki is very persuasive.

I promise her that I would come, er, clean with you regarding my bad breath experience.

It's 9 a.m. on the day of my oldest son Ezra's Bar Mitzvah. My hair is blow-dried, my makeup is done, and I'm wearing a burgundy dress with a floral cardigan. There is beading in the flowers and flowers on my shoes. I am beaming.

Nicki walks through the doors, kisses me hello, and instantly swoops into action. "Your breath isn't so fresh," she says, reaching into her black Chanel purse. She unwraps a stick of blue Extra and slips it into my hand. "Put this in your mouth." This happens so fast, I don't have time to process it. If I did, I would have experienced the following three emotions.

One, dying of embarrassment that everyone who I greeted, two-cheek kissed, and exchanged mazel tovs with, unfortunately had to smell my awful breath, and I had no idea. Two, I had brushed my teeth about forty minutes prior and had eaten nothing since, so why was my breath yucky? Seems unfair. Three, and most of all, thank God I have a sister-in-law who cares enough about me to let me know. Thank God she has the wherewithal — and the chewing gum — to fix this situation, and how lucky I am that she and her husband and kids came all the way from Colorado to celebrate with us.

A few lessons learned from my personal *brush* with bad breath. One, even if you brush your teeth and use mouthwash, sometimes bad breath can triumph. Remember that the person you are talking to may have decent oral hygiene but may just be unlucky. Perhaps aspects of their morning routine need to be revisited (e.g., upgrade their GUM Soft-Picks*), but this doesn't mean that they are fundamentally unclean. Two, the person you're telling about bad breath might appreciate being given a heads-up — like Dave's employee did — so that they can correct the situation. You are doing them a favor because you are letting them know about something that is completely fixable. Three, if you have people in your life who will tell you when you have bad breath, then you are one of the lucky ones. Let's hope whoever you're telling about their bad breath feels that way too.

---

*   Soft-Picks are a new product that my dentist gave me that I put in my makeup case and forgot about until this moment. I promise I'll start today.

19

How to Get Someone to Shower More Frequently Because They Stink

Be Compassionate

On a similar yet not identical note, let's say the smelly cat is your friend, not your employee.[*] And let's say that it's not his breath but his overall — there's no easy way to say this — stink. He makes a killer latte, looks great in jeans, and drives a matte black Porsche Macan. Let's give him a cool alias, Chase. Chase can't for the life of him figure out why he never gets past the first date. You know why — it's his body odor. You have to tell him. He is relying on you as his friend to help him figure out what's wrong, and if you don't tell him, then you are withholding information vital not only to his future but to that of his unmet future bride or groom or other, and his unborn or un-adopted or unfostered future children, one of whom may have

---

[*] *Friends* TV show reference.

gone on to discover a cure for the common cold but now will not be born or brought home because the parents have not yet met because you haven't told your friend he smells like a marathon runner's used shorts, shorts that were left to smolder in the back seat of a taxicab for three weeks. See what I'm saying?

The problem is that body odor sounds a little more personal than fresh breath, and it may take a little more work to fix. Also, it invites responses like "Why are you smelling me?" and you will have to come up with an answer that is not "Dude. People in metropolitan Kansas City are smelling you, and we are 1,300 miles away up in Canada."* Because that would be insulting. And we are not here to insult people, but rather to complain effectively so that we get what we want. And we want to be able to sit in a car with our friend Chase without having to crack the window open, especially when it's 30 below. I don't care if your Fahrenheit trumps my Celsius, 30 below is damn cold by any measure.

So often when we have a friend that smells bad we do everything but actually confront the problem. We offer them shower gels. We buy them deodorant. We go to the mall with them and spend extra long in the bath bomb store. We talk about other people who smell raunchy, hoping they will take the hint. None of this ever works.

Why? Because it's too subtle. It seems obvious to you because you're the one with smells on your mind. But to a regular person who has no idea that they reek, they may think you are highly sensitive to odors, or you're on a scent-based shopping spree. By the way, in this case, our friend might smell because

---

*   But then again, if we were in Canada, we would be smelling in kilometers not miles.

he works out and doesn't shower, or because he's vegan and constantly cooking curries, or because he lives with a room-mate who borrows his soap and leaves you-know-what-kind of hairs on the Ivory, and it's so creepy that he can't deal. There are endless reasons we can come up with to speculate on the root cause of this oniony smell emanating from his every pore.

But we don't need to know why. We need to have the words in our mouths ready so that when this comes up in conversa-tion we are prepared to address it head-on.

Just as with the bad breath example, we need to start by asking if this is our business. If a friend smells bad, you need to dig deep to determine if this pertains to you. Possible convinc-ing arguments for telling someone they stink include these:

- The smell is so out of control you cannot spend time in your friend's presence. You decline invitations to meet up, and you cut him from your birthday list. You don't want to lose him as a friend, and you will if you don't tell him the truth.
- Friend asks you why his dating track record is so poor. It's beginning to affect his mental health, and you fear for his self-esteem and his state of mind.
- Friend is considering a career in fashion sales, and he has asked you to get him an interview at your company. You would love to connect him, but there is no way you can invite him to meet the boss when he smells like canned cat food.

This is by no means an exhaustive list, but, as you can see, each of these scenarios would be enough to determine that telling your friend is indeed your responsibility.

Let's pick a specific example to show a possible entry into

the conversation. Imagine that Chase goes on yet another date. He matched with the woman online, and he thought the texting banter went well. They met for a drink, and she cringed whenever he got too close. She rejected his suggestion of a second date. He doesn't get it. He thinks he has so much to offer. He is slumped on your sofa. You hand him a beer. He says: "Tell me. What do you think it is? What can I possibly be doing wrong? Is it me?"

You have no choice. You have to speak up. Don't worry, though, I am here to help you.

You can say, "Some people are very sensitive to smells. Have you thought about changing your deodorant or going with a stronger body wash?" That might cause Chase to reflect on his hygiene routine, which probably doesn't contain deodorant or body wash, and realize that some serious modifications are necessary.

You can say, "How often do you train? Three, four times a week? Sometimes those odors really linger. Maybe you have to really scrub your workout off so that you smell super clean before you go out." This puts the focus more on the workouts than on his habits, so this might be easier for Chase to swallow.

Third option: Blame an article (or podcast or TV show). "I was reading the other day that with all the plastic and synthetic materials in our environment, people are increasingly sensitive to smells. Apparently, women are attracted to men who smell clean, like a winter forest or a Fiji island.* That might be

---

*   This is an example of the kind of thing one might say to Chase. Please feel free to tailor your remarks to your particular audience, so it could look like "I read that women are more attracted to women who smell citrusy" or "Someone at work told me that men are more attracted to men who smell outdoorsy."

something to consider." And then, if you are feeling bold, you might say, "Lean in here for a sec. Let me smell you. Oh, yeah, Dude, you need to clean this situation up. This is definitely a problem."

You want to be compassionate toward Chase and tell him the truth as nicely as you can, but you also want to be direct so that he gets the message.

Questions for Reflection

1. Do you have any friends who could improve their hygiene? Have you considered whether you are the best person to talk to them about it? Is there anyone else in your friend group that you could run this past or pass this off to?

2. Have you thought about talking to someone about their hygiene, but a little voice has stopped you? Listen to that voice. Is it your fear of confronting the situation? Is it your concern about the other person's feelings? How can you move forward while incorporating these concerns into your conversation?

3. How frequently do you shower? Is body wash a part of your daily routine? Shampoo? It may be a good time to reflect on your personal routine, and make sure you are part of the solution, not part of the problem.

 # How to Get Your Volunteers to Dress More Appropriately

Reframe the Situation

I am dating Dave, and I don't yet know that he is two summers away from becoming my husband. My mom and dad are going to an open-house party, and they would like both of us to attend. They have requested that we "dress appropriately." My boyfriend (Dave) cares more about what they think than I do, and he shows up in khakis, a button-down, a tie, and boat shoes. This looks very appropriate to me, as I lace up my Doc Martens and begin the long task of applying layers of black eyeliner to my lids. My flowered sundress is clean, and it does not have any holes. My mother had a no-hole-in-your-clothing policy that I found very difficult to adhere to when I was a teenager and young adult. Who am I kidding — to this day I am partial to ripped jeans and bleached-out sweaters. I am sad to tell you that my mom passed away a few years ago, and I don't believe she would have supported most of my current fashion choices.

My dad looks at Dave and says, "Are you wearing those shoes?"

Dave is not yet a son-in-law. He responds with a question: "Why? You don't think they're appropriate?"

My dad says, "Well, do you have any other shoes to wear?"

I'm home from college for the summer, and Dave works full-time and goes to school full-time. He lives at home, in the suburbs, about thirty minutes away. It is unlikely that he has packed an array of footwear for this mandatory open house that neither of us understands why we are invited to. He answers in all seriousness, "No. These are the only shoes I brought."

They may well be the only shoes he owns that aren't sneakers. Like I said, he is carrying a full load of classes and running his carpet-cleaning business out of his car. He will eventually sell this business to buy me an engagement ring that I will love, keep in a drawer, and then have reset on our twenty-fifth wedding anniversary, after which I will wear it every day.

He and my father become concerned about the appropriateness of the boat shoes, and brainstorm possible ways Dave can procure different shoes in time for our departure for this open house. Ultimately, they decide that he can borrow dress shoes from his sort-of friend Alexis, who lives two minutes from my house. Alexis doesn't have the same size feet as Dave, but he and my dad decide that newspaper can be stuffed into the toes like my dad used to do when an entire family would share dress shoes and hope they weren't all invited to the same wedding.

I am not happy with this situation for so many reasons. First, I wish my family didn't care what shoes Dave wears, and I wish they would think he looked nice no matter what. Second, I wish that even if they were the types to care, they would be able to put this aside, see that Dave tried his best, and appreciate him. Third, if they had to care, and they were not able to appreciate what he was wearing, I wish they would be able to keep this to themselves, and not encourage him to borrow shoes from some guy in his Intro to Soc class just because he lives down the street and has the closest-possible-size feet.

Also, there is a part of me that wishes my boyfriend could negotiate this situation without feeling like he needs to change and conform to make my parents happy. I have subsequently discussed this with him in gory, gory detail, and I don't think he would stuff his toes with newspaper again, but I think as a boyfriend he genuinely believed he was making me happy too. Even though I clearly said at the time, "Please don't change your shoes. They are being ridiculous. What is an open-house party anyway?"

Eventually, we shuffle off to the party, and, of course, there is a wide array of footwear present, and Dave's boat shoes would not have stood out at all. Also, it never becomes clear why we were invited to this event and why our presence was mandatory that summer afternoon. Other than the shoes, nothing memorable happened. There were no great announcements, no celebrities present, no big reveals.

Also, there were no complaints that day. No one stood up for themselves, no one ordered fries that never came, and, other than my dad asking Dave to change his shoes, no one needed to ask for what they wanted. This story was told to you as historical context to set the tone for this chapter, which is about wanting people to wear something other than what they are wearing, and what baggage I personally carry with respect to this issue.

Which brings us to our next based-in-reality story. Please

put on your workout gear and join me in the hotel gym. I am on the treadmill, and I get to talking with Peter, the complete stranger on the treadmill next to me, who opens the conversation by sharing that he is very active in his neighborhood association.* He has the best posture of anyone in the hotel gym, and his socks are blindingly white. As soon as he finds out I work in complaints, he tells me he has a major problem and needs my advice. One of the key leaders of the association — Kathryn — comes to events not dressed "appropriately."

I ask him to explain.

"You betcha. She wears pants with bleach stains, and her shirt is always untucked. Her hair sticks up all over the place," Peter says. "The other day we had to give an important presentation to City Council about zoning for a dog run that was being built kitty-corner to the garbage dump.† Kathryn came to the meeting in flannel and fleece. Someone needs to tell her that she can't represent our neighborhood looking like that. Any tips on how to do that without hurting her feelings?"

"Whoa. That's a tough one," I say, increasing the incline on my imaginary machine to 3.2. "You're okay with what she says, though, when she represents you?"

"Yes. She is thoughtful and communicates clearly," Peter says.

"Have you spoken to anyone else about this?" I ask.

"Sure have. The other day, Margie, the treasurer of the association, came over to my place with a tuna–tater tot hot

---

* You can tell immediately that this is a fake story because I am never on a treadmill, and if for some reason I do stumble into a gym, the last thing I'd do is have a conversation with someone working out next to me.
† Kitty-corner means the corner diagonally across from the other corner.

dish, on account of my wife was under the weather. Margie says she really likes Kathryn, but her lackadaisical outfits make the whole group of us look bad."

Uff-da.[*] I don't love this complaint. First of all, I am sensitive to judging people by what they are wearing or how they are dressed because I don't always excel at "appropriate" attire. Second, I come from a long line of people who care deeply what people wear and would see nothing wrong with having a guest stuff his toes with newspaper just so that he could borrow someone else's shoes. Third, trying to get what you want, when that includes changing another person, doesn't always work and is usually messy. Like Kathryn's wardrobe.

However, I understand where this guy is coming from. The neighborhood association is going to a lot of trouble to present their case and get certain things changed in the borough. They really want to put their best feet forward, and that includes dressing like concerned citizens who have showered and combed their hair.

I slow the pace on my treadmill and turn to Peter. "I will give you some pointers about how to address this, but on one condition."

He nods.

"I need you to email me and let me know how it all went," I tell him. He agrees. I always ask people to get back to me and let me know the end of the story, and they rarely do, but you know, I have faith in Peter and his spotless white socks.

"You were on the right path when you said you wanted to

---

[*]   Minnesota expression meaning "Oy vey," which is a Yiddish expression meaning "Oh my."

tread carefully," I say. "I suggest you start by asking her some questions."

First, I'm wondering if we know Kathryn very well. Maybe she is a housepainter, and she runs to meetings straight from work with no time to change. Maybe she is a nude model for an oil painting class down at the college, and she doesn't own a lot of clothes. Maybe she used to walk the runway for Donna Karan in the '80s and has shunned fashion ever since. I think the committee members might want to take some time to understand where Kathryn is coming from, and that will help determine how to best address this situation.

The next step is to find out if Kathryn is okay. Maybe she is unwell. Maybe she needs help. Maybe she is suffering from depression, or someone in her family is sick; there may be an explanation outside of the neighborhood association as to why Kathryn is not making pleated pants and twinsets her top priority. If it turns out that things are a struggle for Kathryn right now, and she does feel as if she's underwater, my advice would be to drop the subject of appearances and suggest some practical assistance, such as offering to drive her to an appointment, or finding someone to walk her dog.*

If all is well with Kathryn, I would try to find out if she shares the common understanding of the magnitude of these council meetings. She may see them as less important than the other members of the neighborhood association. I might review with her what's at stake and suggest that we all make the best possible impression by dressing in our Sunday best, or whatever their cultural equivalent is. Maybe Kathryn joined the association

---

* I don't know for sure that she has a dog. I suggest this question be included in the initial get-to-know-you conversation.

because she wanted to meet more people, or she wanted to have a new traffic light installed, and maybe she doesn't have a vested interest in the new dog park. If that's the case, I might subtly suggest that she find her way to another committee, and perhaps leave the council meetings to someone else.

I close my monologue by reminding Peter that sometimes we have to accept people for who they are, and we cannot control what they wear or how they look. I explain to him that women have fought long and hard to have control over our bodies, and that includes our right to make decisions about what we wear. He agrees but adds, "You can't play for the Twins if you don't wear their uniform."

We smile at each other, and my treadmill grinds to a halt. I say good-bye to my new buddy Peter. I remind him of his commitment to keep in touch, slip him a business card, and go on my merry way.*

Three weeks later, I get an email with the subject heading: You Were Right. Peter and Margie went to see Kathryn to have a little chat. Turns out she had been diagnosed with cancer. She joined the neighborhood association to give herself something new to think about, especially since she's now too sick to work. Kathryn didn't want to worry anyone by telling them what was going on with her. Even on posttreatment days, when she can barely lift her head off the pillow, she makes a herculean effort to throw on some soft clothes — hence the flannel and fleece — and head to a council meeting so that she doesn't disappoint the other volunteers. Peter offered to mow Kathryn's

---

* I happen to have my business card with me in the hotel gym. See? That's how you know some details have been changed — aspects of the story just don't make sense.

lawn and drive her to meetings. He also said it would be fine if she missed a few until she felt better. Margie has organized a hot dish train so that Kathryn is never without food she can warm up, if she feels too weak to cook.

"The group of concerned neighbors has in fact become concerned about their neighbors," Peter writes.

Sometimes, when you are asking for something you want, you are requiring the other person to fundamentally change something about themselves. Sometimes, you may recognize that that's impossible, and you may choose to reframe your requirements. In the case of Annie and her spaghetti dinners, we didn't try to get the Betty family to come early, we helped Annie recognize that what she really wanted was for dinner to start on time, which it now does, regardless of Betty's behavior. Here, Peter really wants his neighborhood association meetings to go a certain way, which includes having his volunteers dress "appropriately." While, on the one hand, I believe this is none of his business, on the other hand, I can understand why he wants the group to look organized, efficient, and clean. If one member is not following this principle, and Peter is otherwise happy with her work, then there has to be a way to communicate his needs to her without hurting her feelings.

Because of the delicate nature of the issues — men, women, appearances — I suggested that he kick off by seeing where she's at and making sure she's all right. Turns out she's not all right at all. She is frankly quite sick and can use some help.

Now, imagine what would have happened if I had overslept that day and not gone to the hotel gym. Peter wouldn't have had me to talk to, and he might have addressed this situation by establishing a volunteer dress code or sending out a passive-aggressive email about "clothing expectations," which could have possibly incensed the neighborhood group and caused major friction. And imagine how badly Kathryn's feelings would have been hurt if someone had told her she was not being appropriate when she was actually spending every last bit of energy on just showing up.

When Else to Use This Technique

You can use this technique with a friend who has a behavior you're concerned about. Let's say instead of being too sloppy, your friend is too fanatic about working out. (It's kind of ironic that I staged this conversation in a fake hotel gym, and now I'm saying to use it if you have a friend who you think works out too much.)

Let's say Siena is always at the gym. You feel this is your business because you never get to see her anymore. If you want to hang out with her, you have to encase yourself in black spandex and lace up. (This used to mean something different. Now, it means sweat and tears. Okay, I'm not helping myself. You know what I mean.) Any time spent with Siena has to be on her terms, and you're sick of it. You want her to skip a workout once in a while, and she says absolutely no way.

From where you're sitting comfortably on the couch, Siena's life consists of getting on and off the treadmill, the elliptical, the rowing machine. Maybe she takes three spin classes in a row, and you think she's addicted — either to the endorphins or to the spin instructor's abs. Here's the thing, though — maybe something is wrong. Possibilities include but are not limited to these:

- She is facing huge amounts of stress in her life that she hasn't told you about, and the gym is the only place she can forget about her problems and focus on sweating.

- She suspects her significant other of having an affair. She is either working out before she gets back on the dating scene, or she is hoping to lure her partner back by providing a fit alternative to current dalliances.
- She lost her job and is terrified that she won't find another one. Going to the gym gives her an excuse to avoid the job search market.
- The gym is the only place with free babysitting, and she really needs a break from the kids.
- She feels lost, and the gym gives her a sense of community and people to talk to.

There are so many more possible scenarios that we could come up with — relating to body image, mental health, or other problems that really could use attention.

If you have a friend who is spending too much time at the gym, and you are worried, you need to ask her if something is wrong and if there is anything you can do to help. It may turn out that she is completely fine and has just become all-consumed with her workouts. On the other hand, it could turn out that she really could use a friend to talk to. Please. Look at Siena with compassion, not judgment.

PART III

I Want Justice to Be Served

Part I is about asking for problems to be resolved — things returned, fixed, or improved. Part II is about convincing other people to change so that they smell better, arrive on time, and are more attentive. Part III is about wanting justice to be served so that the world will be a better place, even if there is no personal gain for us. This is assuming that the world will be a better place if umbrella factory workers get the breaks they deserve, and few feathers are ruffled in the process. In other words, we don't necessarily tackle *big* issues in this section, but rather issues that could impact people other than ourselves.

True, this can be said about any situation featuring complaining effectively. Even my green lettuce example at the beginning urges you to speak up so that all the people in line behind you will have greener lettuce too. In that story, we spoke up in enough time to correct the situation so that the lettuce could be replaced, which it was.

Here, we deal with scenarios where the opportunity for personal gain has passed, but we still ask for what we want so that injustice will be corrected. This might mean confronting another mom about her birthday cake selection even if it's too late for her to get another cake today. She will host plenty of birthday parties, and if we speak to her now about our concerns, future invitees will not have to put up with dry cookies. It might mean speaking to a Jewish administrator who is panicking about bacon placement.

These scenarios will help you determine when it's worth speaking up, and what you can say to contribute to global justice on a personal scale.

How to Get Bacon Out of the Synagogue Refrigerator

Collect Data

Here's a food story from Atlanta, Georgia, that does not include boiled peanuts or pimento cheese. It's about bacon. We are at a synagogue conference. A synagogue is like a church except it's for Jewish people, and the services are ten times longer. My husband is active in the synagogue, by which I mean he's president of the whole damn thing, and I am a terrible first synagogue lady, as you can tell already by my use of the words "damn" and "bacon" in the first paragraph of this story.

Dave wanted to go to Atlanta for this conference. I said I would only go if I could speak at it. I proposed a workshop about how to resolve complaints, figuring that a few thousand senior clergy and board members probably hear complaints all the time, and are likely interested in how to solve them.

They gave me a Lunch-and-Learn time slot. I was disappointed because I had to be a good sport and attend the conference as I agreed I would, yet, instead of being in the limelight, I would be presiding over a roundtable of eight to ten delegates, desperately trying to lecture about complaints while the participants munched their pastrami on rye. They will not be eating bacon; that comes later.

I spent the first forty-eight hours of the conference stressing about no one showing up for my talk. I imagined myself having to speak to eight to ten empty seats and my husband. I ended up with the exact opposite problem: four tables smushed together in a packed ballroom so that I had to speak VERY LOUDLY and walk around the tables as I talked so that the forty-plus people attending my Lunch-and-Learn could hear me.

The structure of the talk was the ABCs (and DEFs) of resolving complaints. I started with A — accept that you will hear many complaints in your capacity as chair of this board or that committee — and then I blah blah blah'd until I got to the Q and A.

Someone told the following story and asked for my advice.

A Jewish community agency has several administrators, all of whom have offices on-site and show up for work every day. These people pack their sliced cucumbers into Tupperware to eat at their desks while watching kitten and giraffe videos, just like the rest of us. On this particular rainy morning, an administrator (not the person who is telling the story) goes to put his lunch away. Opens fridge door, hears something oinking at him. Just kidding. Sees package of bacon in refrigerator. Wonders why there is unkosher food in the fridge in a Jewish institution. Administrator feels uncomfortable because Jews are not allowed to eat bacon or any other pig products, and he cannot imagine for the life of him how something like this could have happened.

He panics.

He whips out his phone and takes a picture of the bacon package. Emails the association's clergy, board members, office staff, women's auxiliary, mah-jongg league, softball team, youth group, men's club, and assorted volunteers. Writes long email, some of which is IN CAPS, about the contamination of the fridge, the shock of the experience, and the shame on his family.

"Let me stop you here," I say to the storyteller. "This is a case of asking for what you want *so loudly* that you unnecessarily involve — and disrupt — multiple people."

It would be a lie to say you could hear a pin drop, but people definitely stopped chewing long enough to hear what I had to say.

"When the admin guy saw the bacon, it was time for him to start asking questions," I explain.

He was missing crucial information, such as this:

- Whose bacon is this?
- Why is it in the fridge?
- Where's Jimmy Kimmel?*

Administrator could have discreetly wrapped the bacon in brown paper and stuck it in the back of the fridge while he did his reconnoiter.† No one else would share the traumatic

---

* Jimmy is known for pranking people.
† Also known as a reconnaissance mission, where you send someone ahead to scope things out.

experience of finding contraband sandwich meat sandwiched between the sandwiches.

In fact, several of the email recipients are upset, angry, outraged. They take dietary regulations very seriously, and they have devoted their lives to providing a Jewish-centered environment that wisely avoids bacon.* (Because let's face it, bacon is the gateway drug to prosciutto and other *salumi*.†)

An email battle ensues with vindictive messages flying back and forth while no one actually pauses to directly address the problem. No one stops to ask why this happened. No one calmly posts a note on the fridge reminding users that this is a kosher environment, and pork and shellfish are not welcome.

Instead, a few people threaten to resign from the board. Others circulate a pro–animal rights petition, arguing that no animal products should be consumed on the premises at all. There is a countervegan movement whose slogan appears to be "Chicken soup at all costs."‡

Members demand that security guards check visitors' bags not only for guns and explosives (a tragic consequence of living in these times) but also for bacon-flavored gum.

One of the many email recipients is Shira, on the building and grounds committee. Shira reads the message and remembers approving a separate fridge for employees in the break room. The purpose of the fridge is to allow staff who are not Jewish or do not follow Jewish dietary rules to bring food to work and keep it cold.

---

* Seriously, though, there is a set of Jewish dietary rules called "being kosher," or "*kashrut*," and one of the rules is no shellfish or pig products, which includes bacon.

† *Salumi* are Italian cold cuts.

‡ Joking.

She realizes that this bacon incident may just be a case of mistaken fridge identity. Perhaps a new employee came to work today and put their bacon in the wrong refrigerator. Perhaps an employee capitalized on a bacon sale and stashed his or her rashers in the icebox.

Shira leaves work early, goes to the scene of the crime, and asks the head of custodial services if he knows anything about the stray bacon.

He chuckles and explains that the staff has been surreptitiously looking for the missing meat all afternoon. It seems that one of the kitchen staff brought in a package of bacon for her son, who works at the center and recently moved into his own apartment. The son accidentally put the bacon in the wrong refrigerator. Being new to the job, he didn't realize the sociopolitical ramifications of this maneuver.

The organization ended up having to issue an apology letter to all those involved, reassuring them that the bacon had been relocated and equilibrium had been restored. I can just imagine a patroller circulating through the halls with a bullhorn: STAND DOWN. BACON HAS BEEN RELOCATED. I REPEAT: STAND DOWN. WE HAVE MOVED THE BACON.

All of this could have been avoided had the admin guy waited until he had more information before complaining. Had he just asked around, he would have known that this was not a plot to overthrow the monarchy. Perhaps the administrator should not be so quick to throw his AARP bulletins into the recycling bin. An article in an AARP bulletin a couple of years ago advises: "Whenever possible, talk to an actual person." (Later in the same article, titled "How to Complain," the writer also advises that "often the best approach is to let things go," and not complain about them. However, since that does not add to my point, I'm going to gloss over that piece of advice and feed you only what makes me look like I know what I'm doing.) "Experts say there's a gentler science to making things right when you've been wronged," the article continues, and that's the kind of declaration we are going to keep in mind as we move through the rest of the story.

"Here's what went wrong. The admin guy skipped the data-collection phase," I say to the lunch eaters.

"I'm not a scientist!" Marsha from Atlanta says.* "How do I collect data?"

"By asking questions," I explain. "Let me give you a for instance":

- "I found bacon in the fridge. Is it yours?"
- "Hey, did you see bacon in the fridge this morning? Know whose it is?"
- "Um, we aren't supposed to have bacon in this fridge. Should I throw it out, or do you know who it might belong to?"

Any of these would have led to a quicker and neater resolution than unnecessarily circulating/posting incriminating photos and upsetting lots of innocent people.

When Else to Use This Technique

I feel like this is also a good technique to use at work when something happens that you are unhappy about, like a new mandatory meeting scheduled for Fridays at 3 p.m. Before you fire off a series of steaming emails cc'ing your department,

---

* She later wrote an article about the talk, published in the *Atlanta Jewish Times*, which I only found because I have a Google Alert set for my name, which seems like overkill, but turns out it wasn't.

your boss, her department, and the graphic design staff, take the time to find out what really is happening.

First, I would reread the email or meeting request or any documentation you received directly related to the meeting. Maybe there was an attachment you missed, or a sentence you overlooked, that would provide some background info.

Second, if your search doesn't turn up any clues, ask around and see if anyone knows why this meeting was scheduled and what it is supposed to accomplish. It could be that the boss wants to review where everyone is on Friday afternoons, and if your team's work is complete, she will let you leave at 3:30 instead of insisting that you stay until 5. It could be that new hours will be announced, such as when you add a few minutes to all other days so you can leave a bit early on Fridays. It could be that, technically, your day finishes at 5 p.m., and your boss wants to wring every little bit of productivity out of you.

Third, as in the bacon example, you don't want to fire off scathing emails that might make it look like you are bad-mouthing your boss or undermining her authority. Before you send an email to anyone work-related, complaining about anything work-related, please take the time to informally collect some data, and make sure you have all the facts before jumping to conclusions. Well, you can jump to conclusions in your heart, but I wouldn't publicize them until I knew for sure what was happening.

In-Depth Analysis

Let's go back a step and take a deeper look into the Friday afternoon meeting issue. Let's say your investigation reveals that the boss has decided on these meetings because people have been packing off for the weekend starting after lunch on

Fridays, even though the day technically ends at 5 like every other workday.

You want to ask that the meeting be changed to another day because you find it too stressful to have a major meeting hanging over your head all week. Not that you're necessarily leaving early for the Hamptons / South of France / Netflix, but in the back of your mind, you like to feel that these options are open to you. Here's the thing: The boss is right. You are paid to work until 5 p.m., and she is 100 percent within her rights to require you to go to a meeting at that time.

This doesn't mean that you can't ask for a change; it just means you have to be strategic about it.

I would suggest attending the first Friday afternoon meeting with an open mind and seeing how it goes. If it turns out to be fine, or not as bad as you thought, pour yourself an extra cup of non-decaf, and be grateful you don't work weekends. If the meeting is difficult for you, and you still want it changed, I would speak to the boss about it privately, one on one. If you have regularly scheduled update meetings you can mention it then, or you can drop by and say, "Is this a good time? I want to ask you about something." If she says no, then ask when you can come back, and follow up.

When you are preparing for the conversation, list possible reasons why the Friday afternoon meeting is not the best timing. Perhaps Friday afternoons are busy in your line of work. I know that when I used to work in health care, Fridays, especially the end of the day, were the busiest time of the week and therefore not a good time for meetings. If that's your situation, you can say to the boss, "I understand that you want us to get together weekly, but if I can't be at my desk to greet people / answer messages / sew up wounds, it puts me in a real bind come next week."

If the opposite is true, and Friday afternoons are super quiet, you can try something like "I know it looks like Fridays are quiet, but that's when we catch up on our paperwork, clean out our recycling bins, and wipe down the light fixtures. If we don't have time for that on Fridays, I'm worried that our office will deteriorate."

You can also talk about energy levels, as in: "I noticed the energy level was lower than usual at last Friday's meeting. I'm wondering if we could do it on Wednesdays instead?" Or: "Everyone was so hyper at last Friday's meeting. I'm wondering if we could pick a more chill time to do it, like Tuesday mornings."

Make your suggestions, and then let them sit. Because you are not completely justified in this ask — Fridays are part of the workweek, after all — I don't think you should push. Just offer your suggestions, and then leave them with your supervisor to think about. If the boss never mentions this to you again, drop the subject. This is not an example where follow-up is required. If you can't live with Friday afternoon meetings, and they become a part of the culture at this company, then you may have to consider looking for another job.

 How to Prevent Grandma
from Falling on a Pile
of Broken Pipes

File an Official Complaint

Even if you are the best complainer in the world, you need to make sure you are addressing your issues to the appropriate person. Complaining to your friends from the safety of your couch may be satisfying but ultimately ineffective — you need to figure out who has the authority to correct your situation and let them know what happened so things can improve.

Look how enthusiastic I am about this point. I jumped right into the conclusion or the "lesson learned" without telling you what happened.

Let me back up. My sister and her family recently moved to a friendly street that has block parties organized by a committee. Her neighbor lives in a three-generation home. I'm not sure if this is common in your neighborhood, but Montreal is kind of old-fashioned that way. I grew up across the street from my auntie Arlene and uncle Mattie, and within walking distance of at least a dozen other relatives.

The other day, the neighbor's grandmother fell on the street (*ow*). She tripped over exposed pipes that the city had left out on the sidewalk while doing (endless) repairs. Grandma is not very mobile, and she gets to and from her weekly game of bridge via adapted transport. The transport initiative is a public program intended to help seniors attend community programs, religious events, and five-card stud, even if they have trouble walking. They provide door-to-door service, meaning that the driver is supposed to get out of his driver's seat and walk the client to their house / apartment / geodesic dome.

The adapted van was not able to pull up directly in front of the house because of the huge amount of construction going on. The street was closed to all traffic because the pipes were being replaced on the block. The construction project is so long and complicated that it's not like they can clean up at the end of each day, so there were pipes and cement piles strewn about, making dear ol' Gran's trajectory even more complicated. Ideally, the driver should have parked, put his flashers on, and escorted Grandma to the house, up the three front stairs, and made sure she got in okay. *However.* Unfortunately, the driver observed from his seat at least a block and a half away as Grandma struggled down the street with her cane, and watched her trip over the exposed pipes, landing on — and badly smashing — her jaw while twisting her left wrist, which she used to break her fall. As she crumpled into a pile on the sidewalk and blood spurted from the side of her face, the driver called first his own supervisor, then 911.

Neighbor and her family are understandably furious. They believe this should not have happened. They blame the driver, they blame the construction project, they blame the Mamluk Sultanate Empire of Egypt for inventing the fifty-two-card deck, which made the game of bridge possible. Had the Europeans not brought cards to North America, Grandma would have had nowhere to go today, would not have left the house, and would not have fallen face-first into a pile of concrete. They argue about whether she was mistreated because of her age, her medical condition, or her prior affiliation with a certain garment workers union. But let's keep that last theory between us.

Here's what they all agree on:

- This should not have happened.
- Justice must be served.
- We need to complain effectively so that this doesn't happen again, to Grandma or anyone who relies on adapted transport.
- We need to post this on Facebook.

Family members tap on their screens, composing just the right caption. They tag the city — for leaving a mess. They tag the van company — for leaving her in the street. And, because the neighbor and her family have impeccable manners, they tag the ambulance in gratitude — for racing to help Grandma and gingerly assisting her when the driver arrived on the scene.

This campaign is successful in generating at least 460 comments, piles of dislikes, sad emojis, and at least twenty-two shares.

Another neighbor reaches out to their brother-in-law's college roommate, who is now a cameraman at a local TV station. He knows someone who knows someone, and next thing you know, one of the nephews is booked on morning television to talk about how reckless the adapted transport driver was, how awful the streets are, and how Grandma is in pain but recovering nicely. Several other media outlets pick up the story.

Wow. Pretty impressive. They were able to get close to five hundred comments, people shared this story on their own timelines, *plus* they were booked on television and then radio.

Sounds like a perfect campaign.

And it would be, if all they were trying to do was bring attention to their cause. For example, if your favorite shampoo is being discontinued, you need to get the company's attention and launch a widespread campaign. You would be trying to show that you and a million of your closest friends will be taking your hair-washing dollars elsewhere. That is where social media campaigns are fantastic in making sure your voice is heard.

But social media campaigns are not a substitute for filing a complaint or for speaking to customer service directly. A 2017 article in the *New York Times* advises to "avoid complaining on social media. It may be tempting to blast a company on its Facebook page or on Twitter, but doing so will not necessarily fix your problem." The author suggests that if you must use social media, you are more likely to get results if you post on a site like Yelp or TripAdvisor, which people naturally consult for reviews. I think that's a good point. I would say that media attention can be helpful, but it's only one tool in your toolbox. You may be reaching a lot of people, but none of them have the power to deal with your — or your sister's/neighbor's/grandma's — situation.

I would think of social media complaining as similar to talking a problem over with your friends. Many, many, many friends. Reviewing what happened out loud might make you feel better, and it can help you process your confusion or your shock and sadness. You might enjoy the empathy, sympathy, and attention, which is not a bad thing. What you want to avoid is only yammering to your friends instead of picking up the phone or sending an email and trying to directly resolve the issue in front of you. A 2016 piece in *MoneySense* magazine says it's a widely held truth that the majority of people will post on social media, vow never to shop at that store again, "but they won't ever call customer service to get the issue fixed." I don't want that to be you.

Practicing your complaint out loud to friends, family, or your thirty-two-year-old parrot named Verdi might be useful in putting together the key elements of your complaint letter. And, if you launch a campaign in addition to complaining to the head of the agency, maybe media pressure will help get the appropriate person to act.

Be careful here. If you focus only on Instagram or Facebook complaining, you may get so caught up in your media success that you forget to contact the people who can effect real change. We have a case where an actual person (Grandma) was harmed, and we can insist that a thorough investigation take place. You need to write a letter to someone close to the problem. Options include the manager of the van company, the director of the transport agency, and/or the supervisor of the work crew who left their remnants strewn across the sidewalk.

The purpose of your letter is to notify the transport service of what happened to Grandma and let them know of any lasting effects, such as any injuries she sustained and any short-term suffering, such as a hospital stay. If there was something specific I wanted — for example, a formal complaint against the driver — I would mention it. I might also request a written response to my complaint.

(*Note:* If you would like to take this down a legal path, I highly recommend you consult a lawyer. I am not a lawyer, so I can't comment on the best route to take or not take from a litigation perspective. I am merely giving advice on how to stand up for yourself and/or Grandma.)

Complaining in the media, social or otherwise, is certainly an approach to consider. But it is not a substitute for contacting the source of the problem directly, letting them know what happened, and explaining that they need to fix/improve/change the system so that it will not happen again.

Examples of Possible Correspondence You Could Send

Your first email should go to the transport company to report the incident. Tell them that Grandma was hurt, and find out if protocol was followed. To determine the email recipient, look on their website to see who the general manager is and what their email address is. If there is no general manager listed, look for other job titles that might be relevant, such as supervisor of customer service or director of client relations. If neither of these exist, you can click on the "About Us" or "Contact Us" tabs to get a general email address or phone number. On the phone, say: "Hi. I'm calling because I had an experience with your company that I would like to report, and I need to know who I should email." If they offer to discuss it right here and now, you have two options. If you are ready to report the incident over the phone, you can say yes. If you would prefer to give your report in writing, you can say: "Thank you so much, I appreciate the offer. I would rather send an email to make sure I get all my facts down. Do I send it to you?"

Some people like to cc or copy the whole world in their emails. I'm not sure why. This initial contact is between you and the company, in good faith, with the goals of reporting what happened and asking for more information in return. You can send it to the one or two people who you believe will be able to help you. If you are signing it from yourself and your sister, or your spouse, or anyone else involved, then I would cc them. I would *not* copy multiple people in the company, because it may make you look confused or disorganized.

I am hesitant to give you a template because I don't want you to think there is only one way to do things. Please remember that my words are just a suggestion, and you can modify this example and make it your own. (*Deep breath.*)

SUBJECT: Incident last Tuesday, August 5, 3 p.m.

Dear Ms. Brown,

I hope you are the right person to speak to about this. If not, please forward this email to the correct person, or let me know who I can call.

I am writing to you to report an incident with your adapted transport van that happened last week, Tuesday at 3 p.m.

My grandma, Mrs. Adelaide Smith, was picked up at noon for her lift to the community center. Unfortunately, our street, Wychwood Avenue, is blocked to traffic because of construction. The construction has left considerable debris strewn on the sidewalk and street, and it is difficult for her to navigate with her cane. The driver came to the door and helped Grandma walk to the car, and I felt reassured that she was in good hands and had no concerns about her afternoon pickup. The same van returned to the center to bring her home. This time, the driver waited in the car and let Grandma walk up the street by herself. My grandma could have asked the driver for assistance. On the other hand, I could see where she would be intimidated and not want to cause trouble or be demanding.

From what I understand, Grandma stumbled over some pipes, fell face-first, smashed her jaw, and twisted her left wrist. The driver called 911 but did not get out of the van to check on my grandma or to stay with her. He did not call any family members for her. She was frightened by the pain and the blood on her face, and she lay all alone on the cold pavement until the ambulance arrived.

I'm sure you can understand why the family is concerned and upset about what happened. I have several questions. First, I would like to know what your company policy is regarding road closures. Is the van driver obligated to get out and help Grandma from her front door to the van? And the same in reverse — from the van to the front door? Second, I would like to know whether the driver was correct in calling 911 from the van, or if he should have gotten out to check how she was? Is he qualified to administer any first aid? And third, is it normal that we were not notified of the incident, and only found out because my sister came home early?

Please let me know what you think of this matter. If there is any further information about the incident that you think might be relevant, I would like to hear it. I am available either via email [insert email address] or over the phone [insert phone number].

Thank you for your time.

Sincerely,

[your name]

If the van company writes you back to say that this was a breach of protocol, and the driver should not have left your grandma to walk alone, then you can write back something like this:

SUBJECT: Tuesday, August 5, Incident: Follow-Up

Dear Ms. Brown,

I hope this email finds you well. Thank you for getting back to me with the information regarding my grandmother's file. She is healing nicely, although it will no doubt take her a while to get over the trauma of the fall.

You mentioned that the driver was not following your company policy when he let her walk alone. I am writing to let you know that I would like to file a formal complaint against him so that this doesn't happen to another client on his route. I understand that the construction was not his fault, but I believe his decision to stay in the van played a role in my grandma falling and injuring her face and her wrist.

Please let me know if there is an official channel for complaints at your company, or if this email is sufficient for you to take action.

Thank you again,

[your name]

In addition to this string of correspondence, you may want to write to the city to complain about the state of the street and the way the construction is being handled. Again, consult the website for contact information, and if you can't find anyone who looks like they may be relevant, call and ask who to send your email to.

Here's a sample of this email:

SUBJECT: Incident on Wychwood Avenue, Corner South Street

Dear Mr. Jones,

I am writing to report an incident that occurred last Tuesday, August 5, at approximately 3 p.m. on Wychwood Avenue, just past South Street. As you are no doubt aware, Wychwood has been under construction for six weeks due to the replacement of water pipes. We have complained to the city several times about the debris scattered on our street, and it is my understanding that you have had several conversations with the Neighborhood Association President, Ms. Jennifer Diem.

Unfortunately, the debris led to a serious injury. My 91-year-old grandmother, Mrs. Adelaide Smith, was walking down the street and tripped on a pile of old pipes. She fell, smashed her jaw, and twisted her left wrist.

As you can imagine, we are all shaken up by the incident, and we ask you to please send an inspector to see whether safety regulations are being followed. We need this situation corrected as soon as possible. We are concerned that materials are not being disposed of properly, and it is putting the lives of our residents at risk.

We can all agree that the accident was completely preventable. Had the construction crews cleared the walkway for pedestrians, Grandma would have been able to get home safely.

Please let me know when we can expect to have someone take a look at this situation.

Thank you for your consideration.

Sincerely,

[your name]

The exact content of the letter you write will depend on the specific details surrounding your case. If the neighborhood had been in talks with the city, this would be a good thing to mention. If not, I wouldn't say it. I would just ask for an inspector to come so we could all have a written report showing that there was debris on the street and that it wasn't properly put away. This may come in handy later.

In conclusion, there are many ways to write many different types of letters. My intention is to give you some examples you can modify to suit your particular situation.

How to Get on the Kiddie Coaster with Your Three-Year-Old If You Are Wet and Black

Ask for the Manager

I am at my favorite writing conference, called HippoCamp, in Lancaster, Pennsylvania, and this time I sit down next to a woman who is knitting a pale-blue baby blanket. I tell her how much I love knitting, but I can't knit and take notes at the same time. She says knitting helps her listen to the presentations. We chat on a bit more. She works in education administration, I work in education administration. We both write nonfiction. Her daughter plays basketball, and she always knits at games. My daughter plays basketball too, and I also always knit at games. "Well," she says, "my daughter's black, and she plays on an almost-all-white team. I knit so that I don't embarrass her by calling out." This can't be possible. "My daughter's white. And she plays on an almost-all-black team. She does not want to hear my voice at *all*," I reply. "Also, when she first started to play I may have accidentally yelled "offense" when they were on

181

defense, and that's when I lost my credibility and picked up my knitting needles."

Angie introduces herself and tells me she's sad today because her mom passed away three years ago from dementia.[*]

"You are never going to believe this. Three years ago, *my* mom passed away from dementia," I say. Angie opens her arms, I fall into them, and we've been friends ever since. Angie told me this story about complaining effectively — she has the best laugh — and I told her I need to use it for the book.

Angie and her husband take their three children to an amusement park with a water park area in what I would call the Deep South but is technically referred to as the Rim South.[†] By the way, this is where the similarities between me and Angie end — there is *no way* I would go on anything resembling a roller coaster, and the only reason I survived Space Mountain is because my cousin Douglas swore me a blood oath that once I checked it off my bucket list I would never have to go on another roller coaster again. Ever. As Long As I Live.

In this story, though, Angie and her family focus on the water park. They slide down the Log Jammer, panic through the Raging Rapids, and relax in the Lazy River. They now want to check out the nonwater side of the amusement park. It is a hot, sunny day in July. Angie's husband takes the two older kids on the Roaring Tiger roller coaster, and Angie sets off to find some entertainment for her three-year-old. This little cookie is not very tall, so her options for rides are somewhat limited. They finally find the Pandemonium Pendulum Junior, and they wait in a long, hot line to get to the front. They are still a

---

[*]   Angie is her real name, and she agreed that I use it in this chapter.
[†]   Arkansas.

little waterlogged from the first batch of rides. They are greeted by a young, white, bleached-blonde number, who tells them they can't get on the ride because they're not dressed. They're dressed, but in bathing suits, because they have just been to the water park section. "Nope," Blondie says, "you are not getting on this ride without your clothes." She seems to be taking her job very seriously for someone who is too young to have voted in the last election. True, she is probably just trying to follow the rules. But still.

Angie looks at her little black daughter not being allowed on a ride. She looks at her wallet and sees how much she has spent on this day at the amusement park. She looks into the future and sees herself sitting on a scorching bench with her three-year-old for hours, waiting for her husband and big kids to get back from the roller coaster. She looks in the mirror and thinks about what she needs to do to be able to sleep at night. And then Angie asks to see the manager.

The manager of the ride, an older, also white, male shows up, and says, "You are not getting on this ride without your clothes." Angie says, "Of course we aren't wearing clothes. We have just come from the water park. And by the way, even if we had been wearing clothes, they would be soaked, so what's the difference?"

Angie can't budge him. So she goes to the next tool in her toolbox: "Get me your manager."

There is a shuffle of walkie-talkies and cellphones as an effort is made to find the manager of the manager of the blonde who works the rides at this amusement park. The line slows to a crawl, and Angie has definitely indicated that she means business.

The young, yellow-haired honey who operates the ride

lights a cigarette and fiddles with her necklace. The sun bounces off the shiny metal ride onto all the people in line. Angie is not going to walk away from this.

The manager of the manager of the manager of the necklace fiddler shows up and says to Angie, "You are not getting on this ride without your clothes."

"We are wearing bathing suits," Angie says, "because we were just at the water park side of *your* park. Now we want to go on the other rides, which are included in the ticket price."

The manager's manager does not know what to do. He straightens the collar on his golf shirt and folds down the pleats of his khaki shorts. He looks down at the long line of people. He then looks at Angie and her adorable daughter, and says, "Ma'am. What do you want?" The subtext here is: What will make you shut up? What will make you go away? I'm in no mood for a full-scale protest, especially by a black woman, because that will not reflect well on me or this park.

"Well. If I can't get on this ride without a T-shirt, then get me a T-shirt," Angie answers. Her subtext is: If you are going to make unreasonable rules and enforce them only sporadically, then you'd better be prepared to cough up complimentary T-shirts.

The third- or fourth-level manager rolls his eyes, exasperated. "Fine."

"There are five of us, though. Bring us five T-shirts."

The line resumes its normal pace, and the managers locate five T-shirts. Angie and her daughter each put one on immediately, saving the remaining three for when they reunite with the rest of the family, so they will all be appropriately clad for the dry part of the park.

This incident gets woven into the fabric of Angie's family

history, and the expression "Don't get all T-shirt" becomes code for "Don't go bananas and keep escalating until they run out of managers to send us."

In certain select circumstances, escalating the complaint can get you what you want. This is not my first choice for advocating for yourself, but in some cases like this one you may not have many options.

Angie's complaint worked for a few reasons. First, she made it clear that she meant business and was not going to take no for an answer. She explained that people were wearing everything from surf shorts to shorty shorts, and so it was very difficult to discern what constituted actual clothes and what did not, like a bathing suit. Still, her voice was not being heard, so she asked for a manager.

Second, Angie did not scream and yell. She calmly asked for a manager. And another manager, and another, until someone showed up who could actually solve the problem. If Angie had been shrieking irrationally, I doubt her outcome would have been so successful.

Third, Angie modeled effective complaining for her daughter. She didn't give up. She showed that it's possible to complain and keep your dignity. And get free T-shirts.

Please note that like all the tips in this book, this one is not good for every single situation. Sometimes we are too fast in demanding to see a manager. If the person in front of you has the ability to help, and you are asking to see their supervisor, it's a clear indication that you are not interested in working with them. I worry that this can backfire in two ways. If the supervisor is not available and you have broken the front-line person's trust, then they may not be as interested in helping you. Or if the person in front of you has a great relationship with the supervisor, they may whisper something about you being difficult or irritating, and this may impact your ability to get what you need. Before you ask to see the next level up, consider your timing.

Alternate Universe Analysis

I can't help but wonder how this situation would have been different if Angie and her daughter were in a northern state, or if any of the people working at the amusement park were people of color, or if Angie and her daughter were not. Race in America is so complicated and at times ugly. I have no ideas or solutions or balms to soothe the ache. I also don't have any delusions about how challenging, difficult, and, at times, enraging, racism is.

Someone once told me that the best way for me to understand race is to imagine all Jews as blue-skinned. I have two thoughts about that. One, how great would my graying hair look against a blue complexion? Two, the blue-skin idea pops into my mind when I am on the subway or at a work meeting or at a Jewish community event. It reminds me that, even though I feel that I wear my culture on my sleeve, the truth is I don't.

Does this mean that Angie and her daughter would have been greeted with open arms and escorted onto the ride on palomino stallions if they were white-skinned? Probably not. Does it mean that their blackness played a part in at first being denied their request and then continuing to have to argue until the management realized she meant business? Probably.

Fact is, we can't read this story without acknowledging that race plays a part in our ability to stand up for ourselves. Maybe Angie feels blacker when she has to argue with a white necklace fiddler half her age about letting her three-year-old on a kiddie ride in a bathing suit. Maybe I am self-conscious about writing this book knowing that Jews are often portrayed as aggressive bigmouths, and here I am, yapping again.

Take a moment, and think about how this pertains to you — your race, culture, class, and outward appearance. Acknowledge that race, age, religion, and number of face piercings can all play a part in how you are perceived. Ask yourself if this has an impact on your ability to advocate for yourself. Think about ways this can help or hurt you going forward.

24

How to Get Your Coworkers to Clean the Kitchen

Be More Threatening

Please meet Claudine. She works in a factory with conveyor belts and other industrial machinery, and she knits the most delicate lace shawls you've ever seen. Her job is to fix the equipment as soon as it breaks, so she spends most of her time on call, waiting for something to go wrong. That's how she got involved in lace knitting — something will always go wrong. Just kidding. She got into lace knitting to challenge her mind with all the downtime and the waiting around that her job involves.

I was introduced to her at a knit-along class at Espace Tricot, my fabulous local yarn store. We were knitting-along a knee-length cardigan with a lace yoke and lace sleeves. Claudine likes her job, but she has a problem with the kitchen on her warehouse floor. The kitchen is always dirty.

Her coworkers leave their coffee cups and yogurt spoons

in the sink. They leave crumbs in the microwave. Plastic baggies of liquid cucumber lie flattened in the fridge, nestled against takeout containers that were never properly sealed. There are enough science experiments in the fruit drawer to keep all ten Horatio Alger Honeywell Scholars occupied for a full year.* Messy coworkers can be the worst if you're a neat freak. Even a moderately sanitation-minded person who shares a kitchen with a messy coworker or two can easily lose her mind.

When Claudine asks for my advice, she believes she has tried everything. She has left up signage with slogans like "Your mom doesn't work here. Please clean up your own mess." Which, by the way, as a mom, I find offensive. Why is it part of my job description to wash anyone else's coffee cup? Maybe it should say, "Are you staying in a five-star hotel? Your maid service is canceled for today. Please wash your own cups."

"I am at the living end of my rope," Claudine says. "I love this job. The opportunity to fix high-frequency vibrating screens as soon as they break is fantastic.† But I might end up having to quit because of the messy kitchen."

Claudine has also posted notices on the fridge like this one: "PLEASE NOTE: The fridge will be cleaned on Monday, October 15. Anything not removed by that date will be thrown out. This includes bento boxes and Tupperware!" This is passive complaining. We may need to introduce some more active complaining techniques.

"Oh, Claudine, I feel your pain, and I have even more bad

---

*   Honeywell has a competitive scholarship program that awards money for students in science, technology, engineering, and math (STEM) subjects.

†   These screens are used in mineral-processing factories to separate this from that.

news to break to you. The signage you put up does not appear to be working. No one is going to change their behavior because of a yellow sticky note plastered on the lid of their festering tuna salad, or a sheet of photocopy paper on the outside of the fridge. It's very easy to tune out messages that sound — I'm sorry, but I have to be honest — naggy and annoying," I tell her.

Claudine has to speak up and tell her coworkers that they need to clean the kitchen. The best way to communicate a message like this is to catch a person in the act and address the situation immediately. Claudine does not need to go undercover in a rented minivan painted to look like a repair vehicle and park down the street. I'm thinking of a simpler stakeout, which would include a bit of extra loitering in the kitchen. When someone puts their cup in the sink, she can say something like "Are you looking for a clean sponge? It's in the drawer to your right." Other possible lines: "What do you think of the green apple–scented soap? I kinda like it." Or: "I'm so glad you're washing your cup out. I hate to see the dishes pile up in there." In all those cases, Claudine is gently encouraging the person to wash their cup without being too aggressive or accusatory.

While the person is washing their cup, Claudine can expand her reach. She can open the fridge and say, "Is that blue container yours? I think it's expired." Or, "Do you drink milk or cream?" And depending on what the person answers, she can say, "Looks like the milk's gotta go," or, "The cream spilled all over the place; you probably should clean it up."

If that plan doesn't work, Claudine can speak to her manager or team lead about the situation. Here's the hard part, though. Claudine needs to be direct, but she can't make it sound like she is accusing everyone. Her best chance of getting results is acting like it's a problem that absolutely must be solved because the consequences can be dire. She can say to the manager, "Have you seen the kitchen lately? It looks like the high school cafeteria in a bad '80s movie. We may need to do something before a VP passes by to make herself a coffee." Or, "Wouldn't it suck if we lose our ISO certification because the kitchen is so dirty? I heard that the inspectors go through every aspect of the floor, even the kitchen." She can talk about the threat of bugs or vermin: "I hope that wasn't a rat under your desk the other day. Might've come from the kitchen. When's the last time you were in there? It needs a thorough cleaning."

If none of this works, or if the manager is one of the offenders, then Claudine can ask to be put on the agenda for the next team meeting. At the meeting, she can ask everyone to clean up their stuff, again mentioning possible ramifications, such as "At my friend's company, they closed the kitchen and took away the coffeemaker just because they weren't cleaning up. They've been stuck with chamomile tea packets for three months."

Now, let's promote Claudine to manager. She has all the same strategies, yet people are still not listening to her. Now she could call employees into her office one by one and say, "The kitchen is dirty. This is not acceptable. I need you to wash your cups and dishes when you're done, and take your lunch remains with you at the end of the day."

Then, depending on the policy at this particular company, she can add something like "Please consider this your first warning. After this, you will get a letter in your file." The employee is likely to be upset, and to say that their ability to keep their kitten mug sparkling clean is not a part of their job description. If that happens, Claudine will answer, "Your ability to look after yourself and your surroundings is an integral part of any job description. Also, your lack of responsibility in this matter is a concern to me, and to the company."

The employee may deny involvement. In that case, I might consider pulling together the group of people who use the kitchen and explaining that they will each be given a specific mug and a location in the fridge that they are responsible for.

I don't usually flip a story to the negative side, but in this case, I think it may be useful to look at the advice that I *haven't* given Claudine. First, I don't think Claudine should wash all the dishes and clean everything herself. This would make her upset and ultimately resentful, and it would come to be expected of her. Claudine, if you have been doing all the kitchen cleaning to avoid facing the ugly truth, please stop immediately.

I don't think that improving the signage will make a difference. Even if the notes have more relevant slogans or cuter pictures (sorry, Snoopy), I'm not sure they will have a greater impact; therefore, I don't suggest adding any new ones.

Finally, it appears that these coworkers are inconsiderate. Therefore, I don't think that saying things like "The mess really bothers me" or "Your filth makes me sick" will encourage them to change their ways. This looks like a case where external pressure due to actual consequences needs to be applied, like the threat of an infestation of vile bugs, or losing an important quality certification.

In the end, I never finished the cardigan. I ended up frogging the whole thing* and putting the yarn back in my stash for further use. And Claudine ended up convincing her coworkers that they had to keep the kitchen clean or face potentially dire circumstances, such as life without a coffee machine.

---

* When you rip out your knitting, it's called *frogging* because "rip it, rip it" sounds like "ribbit, ribbit."

As with the other advice I've given you, I expect you to make it your own. Use words and examples that make sense in your industry and your world.

Alternate Universe Analysis

Let's say Claudine tries all of this, and nothing works. No one cares about the filthy kitchen, the potential for vermin infestation, or the threat of losing a quality certification. She tries everything in her arsenal and gets nowhere. Claudine still has a few options.

First, she can look for a new job. I know this sounds a bit melodramatic, and maybe unnecessary if everything else is going well. However, if the kitchen situation is so aggravating, and it accurately reflects the (lack of) collaboration and cooperation of her coworkers, then maybe it's time to pack up her rosewood and/or carbon-fiber knitting needles and find some new machinery in need of repair.

Or Claudine can put on her hazmat suit and cope with the kitchen filth, pampering herself daily with self-love, self-care, and positive affirmations. Oh, and a whole whack of plastic wrap to double- or triple-wrap her food.

If Claudine loves everything else about her job, and the only problem is the disgusting kitchen, she can create a little kitchen of her own, at her desk, that would circumvent her need to share space with her coworkers. She can pick up a mini fridge for her office or cubicle and get a coffee-pod dispenser or electric teakettle for her desktop. She can scrub all her spoons in the bathroom sink to her heart's content and never set foot in the kitchen again.

How to Call Out Another Mom for Suboptimal Cupcake Behavior

Speak Up Even If It Hurts

We are at a birthday party at the local suburban community center. The guests have frolicked in the mat room, played with trucks and blocks, and have now assembled for cake and juice. The guest of honor is turning three, so the majority of invitees are between two and four years old. Each has a parent with them because they are too little to fend for themselves. Most of them can barely speak.

The birthday boy is at the head of the table. There are balloons tied to his chair and a party hat on his head. He is grinning. The lights go off. There is a sharp intake of breath, because in their twenty-four months on this earth, these humans have already learned that when the lights go out, it means cake is coming. The mom brings out a giant cupcake, dripping with white icing and colored sprinkles. There are candles in it. Everyone sings "Happy Birthday." The birthday boy blows out the candles. His mom lets him dig into the giant cupcake.

She then takes a platter of dry bakery cookies and passes them around for the other children.

"That's strange. I wonder why she is giving them cookies before their cake?" says the mom next to me.

"Yeah, I've never seen that before. A cookie appetizer," I answer.

A few minutes pass as Mom and Grandma take pictures of the boy smearing icing on his face and digging into his giant cupcake. Then it hits us. Our kids are not getting any cupcakes. This mom brought one cake only for her own kid, and she is fine with our kids having crumbly cookies. Like I said, they are two or three years old.

It doesn't take long for the kids to point to the massive cupcake and start saying, "I wan' dis," "Want cake," and "Cake mine?" Some of their eyes are welling up. Parents are crouching next to tiny tables and chairs, trying to explain something that doesn't make sense. You have been brought to a birthday party, yet you will not receive any cake. True, the honoree has been gifted with the biggest cupcake any of us have ever seen, but there is none for you.

In the moment, this problem is not fixable. The mom has not brought cake for my kid, or for any of the twenty or so other kids around the table. It's not like if I pointed this out to her, she'd be able to remedy the situation immediately. I have no birthday cake in my purse. There is no birthday cake service down the hall, or bakery down the street that she could run to and get an extra cake in under five minutes. Like I said, we are at a suburban community center. Any other acceptable birthday cakes are a car ride away.

I am seething and unable to keep my mouth shut. On behalf of moms and kids everywhere, I can't run the risk that this woman does something like this again. I partially blame the community center, which should have clear guidelines for acceptable party refreshments. If they are unambiguous about insisting that we take off our shoes in the gym and that all face-painting be booked through Marsha's Magic, they can also ask for equitable treatment for everyone present. Fresh coffee for the adults wouldn't hurt, either.

One by one, around teeny tables, parents explain to their kids that they can have cake (or ice cream or fruit roll-ups or whatever the bribe of choice is in that family) when they get home / get in the car / get to the grocery store. The kids are so little that this doesn't work 100 percent, but some of the babies definitely calm down. They put on their coats and boots faster than you can say "Canadian winter," and before you know it, they are stomping across the snowy parking lot to their mini-vans.

I am taking my time in the party room, schmoozing with the remaining parents, and letting my kid play a little longer than necessary. I am waiting until the room clears to say something to this mom. I don't want to embarrass her in front of everyone, and at the same time, I cannot let the cupcake injustice go. I am so outraged that she would think it's okay to provide a special, A+ dessert for her own kid, while treating the guests like second-class citizens.

I convince myself that by explaining to her that what she did was wrong, I am doing her a favor. This is her first kid. And this is my third kid. I have been to more of these birthday shindigs than any of us would like to count. She is just starting out on the circuit — a debutante, if you will.

I wait until the room has cleared, and she is wrapping up what's left of her son's massive dessert, and I say to her, "I know this is your first kid, and I'm sure you didn't do this on purpose, but in the future, you really need to get the same dessert for the whole class."

"What do you mean?" she asks.

"Well, you got a jumbo cupcake for your kid — it looked phenomenal, by the way — and all the other kids thought they were getting jumbo cupcakes too. Even miniature cupcakes would have been fine. But they ended up with dry, crummy cookies, and I don't know if you noticed — a few of them were crying," I say.

The mom does not take this well. She starts to raise her voice at me. She starts to scream and yell about how overwhelmed she is, about how hard it was for her to pull this together, about how everything she does is wrong, everything she touches is ruined. She brought the other kids cookies, for which they should be grateful; she didn't have to bring them *anything*. The cake was only for her kid because he's the birthday boy, he's the important one here, and then she finishes with, "THERE! Is *this* going to make you happy?" and she takes the remainder of the giant cupcake and dumps it into the trash.

Oh. That did not go as well as I thought it would in my head. I imagined that she'd be a little embarrassed, maybe apologetic, and ultimately see my point. I did not have any indication that she was holding on by a thread and that this party was the best she could do under what were clearly trying circumstances. I am sorry that this mom is having a rough time. I am also sorry that no one — ranging from the server in the bakery to the community center party planners to her own mother — explained to her that it is in poor taste to give your kid a visibly superior dessert at his own party.

I pack up my kid and leave.

I have very little to do with this mom, and the air between us never gets cleared.

Years and years later, I sit down in a crowded movie theatre, and who is opening a water bottle on my left? Cupcake. "I think of you often," she says to me.

I duck, and fumble in my purse for anything that will disguise my identity. Too late.

"You taught me an important lesson," she says. "You were right. I should have gotten the same cupcakes or cake for all the kids. I didn't even think of it. I was so in my own head that I didn't realize what I was doing. Thank you for pointing out to me how unfair it was. I never did anything like that again."

This story carries with it two lessons. The first lesson is that even when you can't correct something on the spot, it may still be worth giving your feedback so that it doesn't happen again. In this case, I was correcting an injustice not just for my cakeless kid but for all the other kids who would attend birthday parties hosted by this mom in the future. The second lesson is that even if something is not well received at the time, it doesn't mean that your complaint was ultimately ineffective. It turns out that this mom, once she had a chance to think about it, realized that there was merit to what I was saying.

The other issue we have to address here is that, as people, we need to be kind to each other. It could be perceived that by calling out this mom about her lack of cake-shopping skills, I was judging her or making her feel inadequate. I can see that side of the debate, but let me defend myself. Here's what I did to mitigate the damage:

- I waited until everyone was gone so that I didn't embarrass her in front of them.

- I acknowledged that there was nothing we could do about it now, and that I knew she didn't do it on purpose, so I gave her a built-in out.
- I told her in person and didn't send a judgy email or text.
- I didn't take pictures and post on my timeline, or refer to it on any social media platform.
- From her initial reaction, I learned that she was having a rough time, and I backed off immediately.

Therefore, I conclude with the belief that I did the right thing — even though it was a bit difficult to watch, especially when she threw the remainder of the you-know-what into the trash.* Sometimes speaking your mind can be a challenge, but I ultimately believe it's usually worth it.

When Else to Use This Technique

This is a good technique for when you see someone you know doing something wrong, and you have an urge to correct it, but you want to do so without causing a scene. Let's take the example of a nonhandicapped person parking in a handicapped spot without the correct sticker or license plate. For this to make sense, it would have to be someone you know, because there are all kinds of disabilities that merit the sticker but are not instantly visible to the naked eye (e.g., chronic diseases, extreme pain, etc., depending on where you live and what the regulations are). If you suspect misuse of the space, you can ask

---

* Was I tempted to fish the cupcake remains out of the trash and give them to my own kid? Possibly. But I'm proud to say I resisted the temptation, and dignity won out over vanilla frosting.

the parker if everything is okay, and if the person answers that they are in a rush and will only be using the spot for a second, you may feel justifiably incensed.

You are tempted to take pictures, and post them all over social media, tagging the offender. You compose a scathing text message in your head. You draft a vitriolic email, extolling the virtues of handicapped parking and the injustice of using the spot when your mobility is not impaired. But then you look around the parking lot and see a pile of three-year-olds having crumbly cookies while one smug birthday boy stuffs his face with white icing. In other words, you remember this story. You look the offender right in the eye, and you say something like this: "I know you are in a rush, and you didn't mean to take up a parking spot, but these are reserved for handicapped people who really need them." Or: "You know, I never used to take handicapped signage seriously either, until I saw someone with a cane struggling across the parking lot because all the reserved spots were filled. Damn near broke my heart. Do me a favor — next time, please park somewhere else so that people who really need the spots could get to use them."

I could go on with suggestions, but I think you get the point. Voice your concerns in person. Try to do it when you don't have an audience. Be calm and clear. If you see the person is getting very upset or angry, it's okay to back away. You have made your point.

# How to Accidentally Get Your Waiter Fired

Rise Above the Fear

For the first part of my career, I worked in health care on the administration side. I worked in patient safety, which is a polite term for medical mistakes. I worked on quality improvement and measurement, as a senior manager of a bunch of departments, and also as an ombudsman. In those years I developed several workshops including one titled "How to Say I'm Sorry in the Workplace." I went around to the patient or client care units and spoke to the frontline nursing staff about saying I'm sorry, and once, in an attempt to be reassuring, I accidentally said something like "Don't worry, heads aren't going to roll for this."

Hindsight being 20/20, I can see where the imagery was possibly a bit too graphic for the occasion and the audience. For a head to roll, it has to be violently hacked off the body in a bloody and painful death. *Oops.*

Luckily, my boss and the rest of my team had a decent amount of faith in me, and my head didn't, er — well, nothing drastic happened to me as a result of inappropriate phrasing. I was given a chance to continue workshops with the staff as long as I struck that particular comment from my speaking notes.

I also avoid mentioning heads rolling when I'm trying to reassure people who are deciding whether to formally complain. Even when we have been wronged, many of us are reluctant to speak up because we don't want someone to lose their job because of us. Yet, people do not lose their jobs as the result of one complaint. If you are the first to complain about someone, they might get a conversation or a warning. Or they may get nothing whatsoever. The management may listen and be polite to the complainer (you), but they may believe that their employee has done nothing wrong, and if it's a first infraction, they might be willing to ignore it.

I still think it's worth complaining about suboptimal service. If you're the first one to have this problem with an employee, one of two things will happen. Possibly, the manager will have a gentle conversation with the person that will result in correcting the situation for the next time. Or the manager might just mentally file your issue under "important things to know about my employees." The second time someone complains, the manager will rifle through his or her mental filing cabinet, and see that this has happened before and needs to be taken more seriously this time. But if you say nothing, the next time someone comes along there will be no precedent. Makes sense?

The other day, my dad was talking to a friend of ours who owns two hotels in Belize, one near the beach and one in the

Belizean rain forest jungle, neither of which I've been to but both of which sound idyllic, and they got to talking about challenges with employees in the tourist industry, like the time my parents visited Greece in the late 1960s.

Let's roll the tape.

My parents are in a small town in Greece. It is hot and summery, and everything is white. They are sitting outside at a *taverna* ordering grilled fish — *kalognomes*, a type of shellfish from the Ionian Sea, with tomatoes and olives. They drink wine. They look at the view. They also order carefully, taking into consideration what my grandpa Henry called the "right side" of the menu* because even though they are in this exotic location, they are still only a few years out of law school and teacher's college, and while they don't have to pinch pennies, they certainly have to keep track of their money.

The bill comes.

My dad reads it carefully. Thirty-eight years later he will become a justice on the Supreme Court of Canada, and this level of attention to detail will serve him very well, but we don't know that yet. Now, we see him confused about the bill as it comes to way more than he expected — in fact, probably double what he was expecting — and while I agree that he's in another part of the world, math should be transferable.

"Excuse me?" my dad says to the waiter. "Can you please explain to me where these prices came from?"

"Just pay, you pay," says the waiter, smiling at my parents, perhaps seeing them as fat Canadian fish he has hooked.†

"I'm not giving you my money," my dad says reasonably as

---

* The right side of the menu is where the prices are.
† Fat in terms of money, not blubber.

my mom freshens her coral-pink lipstick, "until you explain to me why this meal costs more than the prices listed on the menu."

The waiter, who had been chatting amiably in English all through dinner, appears not to understand what he is saying, leaving my dad with no choice but to get out of his painted white wooden chair and speak to the manager.

The manager looks at the handwritten bill in my dad's hands. My dad shows him that they have been charged double for their grilled *kalognomes* and salad of fresh tomatoes sprinkled with oregano. The manager agrees that this is indeed strange; however, he confides, this is not the first time their waiter has pulled a stunt like this, and he has no choice but to "take care of it."

"Look," my dad says, "we don't want him to lose his job. We just want our bill corrected."

"*Nai*," the manager says, which means "yes" in Greek, although it sounds suspiciously like "no."* My dad reaches into his cargo shorts for his *drachmas* and pays the manager according to what the menu says, not according to what was on the bill.

My parents walk out of the restaurant, concerned that the server will now lose his job because of them, but also vindicated. They have been told that he has pulled this stunt on other tourists, and their speaking up was the last straw.

The next morning, my parents leave on a cruise of Delos and some other islands, and the taverna, white-painted chairs, and almost-overpriced *kalognomes* are forgotten.

---

*   "No" is "oxi" (*o-chi*), which sounds sort of like "okay," so please be careful about what you agree to when traveling through that part of the world.

The boat trip — I may be giving it too much credit by calling it a cruise here, maybe it's a tour — lasts a few days, after which they return to the same town, and walk up the hill to their hotel. The sun is beating down, and my mom can't wait to get into a proper shower and rinse the boatiness off her body.

However, the splash of cool water on hot skin will have to wait a few minutes because, who is waiting for them in their hotel lobby?

The waiter!

"Please!" he begs on one knee, suddenly fluent in English. "You must help me! I lost my job! My wife is going to leave me! I can't support my kids! I am desperate! I need your help."

My dad experiences the following mixed emotions:

- *Surprise:* He would never have expected the waiter to track him down, find out where he was staying (it must have been a very small town), and wait for him in the hotel.
- *Fear:* If the waiter is so desperate, who knows what lengths he'll go to? My dad does not want trouble.
- *Irritation:* My mom wants to take a shower, and my dad wants my mom to be happy, and this guy is getting in their way.
- *Disappointment:* He specifically told the manager that he didn't want the waiter to lose his job because of this interaction, and the manager apparently had his own reasons for letting him go anyway.

Dad handles the situation by chatting with the waiter for a few minutes, figuring the principle of "some people just want to be heard" might work here. The waiter asks my dad to come back to the restaurant with him and ask the manager for his job back. If the internet had been invented, I might have wondered if the waiter figured out that my dad was a criminal defense attorney by profession and was well qualified to plead for a lesser sentence on his behalf. However, the waiter could not possibly have known this information; he was just asking my parents for help even though he was the one who had attempted to dupe them by falsifying their bill so that he could pocket the difference.

In all his hotel lobby begging, he never denies having committed the crime. He just believes he shouldn't be punished for it.

Ultimately, the hotel staff escorts him out, my parents are scheduled to fly home the next morning, and no further drama ensues.

However, we know a few things for certain. One is that my dad will read this chapter and send me a list of all the things that didn't happen as I described them. For instance, my mom may not have been wearing lipstick that day, or they may have had pearly razor fish instead of grilled *kalognomes* for dinner, and it may have been fried, not grilled. Dad, I tried my best to reconstruct a story that you told me in colorful detail, and I am sorry if some of my embellishments do not match exactly to how things truly unfolded.

Another thing we know for sure is that my dad was 100 percent right to ask for what he wanted — an accurate bill. He should not have had to pay double for his meal just because he was worried that someone he never met before might get in trouble for trying to cheat him. Cheating is bad behavior, and people who deliberately attempt to fleece others deserve sanctions. Yes, the severity of the sanctions and the process by which they are meted out may be subject to discussion and conversation, but I am completely convinced that an incident like this should not go unreported. Especially since my dad tried to clear things up directly with the waiter. Had the waiter just backed down and apologized for the miscalculation, he'd have been on his way to work the next day.

One lesson is that it is tempting to think about everyone else and the consequences that will befall them when we ask for what we want (like an accurate bill). But remember that you did not ask the waiter to falsify the bill. If you say nothing and pay what you don't owe, you are letting him think he can do this to the next person. And if they stay silent, the next person. And so on. It is very rare for someone to lose their job because of one misstep. If it happens, as we see here, it's because your complaint is the last straw.

Another lesson is that some people might feel guilty that the waiter has children, and he says he can't support them now that he's lost his job. *Just a reminder:* He lost his job because *he cheated*, not because *my dad spoke up*. Had he not committed a crime, my dad would not have reported him, and he would be feeding his family as we speak. Also, we don't have all the facts here. We don't even know if the waiter has children — he has already established himself as a liar, so I'm disinclined to believe anything he says. We don't know if he can't feed them because he has already been fired from several jobs for the same petty crimes, or if he was recently released from prison for a serious crime. We don't know whether he lost the family savings on a harebrained mining scheme, or whether he spent all he has on a giant-screen TV (which has not been invented yet). How this guy ended up living paycheck to paycheck would require a detailed investigation that is not part of our responsibility when we speak up. What we have to worry about is whether we've been wronged (i.e., given a deliberately doubled bill).

I started out this chapter by saying that heads rarely roll in the world of speaking up for what you want or need. I am now amending this to say that in the event that someone does lose their job, it's because of a whole host of reasons (such as attempting to steal from you), not because you pointed out the problem. Oh, right, I'm not supposed to talk about heads rolling — it makes people uncomfortable. *Oops.*

Sorry.

Questions for Reflection

1. Have you ever questioned the accuracy of an invoice or bill? Think about what would cause you to go to the manager. Is it because you are 100 percent sure you were being fleeced? Or are you the type who would bring forth a concern on suspicion alone? How much proof does one need to ask the manager to check pricing?

2. If you came back to the hotel, and the server was waiting for you, would you be frightened? I would, for sure. Would you stop and talk to the person? Would you walk right past them? I think it's unlikely that this would happen in today's day and age, but maybe you would get a Facebook message from a server or hairdresser or tai chi instructor who you questioned and who tracked you down. Take a minute to think about your personal boundaries, and how far you would go to have or avoid a conversation.

3. What are your thoughts on the expression "Heads will roll"? Does it sound violent to you? Think about other expressions we use without thinking, and how they may sound to others. Are there any words that you would like to clean out of your conversation? When are you going to start?

 # How to Get the Break You Deserve at Work

Know Your Rights

My seventeen-year-old son, Benji, got a job working in an umbrella factory. Not really, but I want to disguise his actual place of business, and once, when I was a sophomore in college, my Italian professor showed us a video of an umbrella factory, and it has stuck with me to this day as an intriguing subject for a documentary, an interesting Italian lesson, and now a fake place of employ.

One of the things Beno likes best about his new job is that the schedule is variable. He doesn't have to have the same hours every week. Depending on his school workload, his hacky-sack commitments, or his Humans 4 Humanity* meeting, he can submit different availabilities, which means he can work different days every week.

---

* Humans 4 Humanity is a nonprofit that works toward social justice globally and locally.

This also means that the shifts are not always the same hours or the same length of time. The umbrella factory is open until 11 p.m. Which does not make sense, until you remember that it is not really an umbrella factory but rather an umbrella factory in disguise. Benji sometimes works four hours, sometimes six hours, rarely — but it could happen — eight hours.

The manager tells Benji that for every four hours he works, he gets a thirty-minute break. Today, he is scheduled for a five-hour shift. He clocks in at 1 p.m. At 2 p.m., his coworker tells him to go take his break now — things are slow. Benji is new and wants to get along with everyone, so he does not ask any questions. He takes off his umbrella factory safety equipment and heads to the break room, where he takes out his sliced turkey and Jarlsberg on an onion roll and scrolls through his phone.

Break passes all too quickly, and Benji is back upstairs, safety shoes and goggles on, and he is making umbrellas. The manager summons him to his office at the back. Benji nervously shuffles in behind him.

"Were you just taking your break?" he asks.

"Y-y-yes," Benji answers.

"You're working 1 p.m. to 6 p.m. today?"

"Y-y-yes," Benji answers.

"I thought I explained to you that you need to work four hours to get a thirty-minute break?"

"Yes, sir," Benji answers. "I'm working five hours today, so I get a thirty-minute break."

"Benji. I'm not going to write you up because you're new

around here, and you look like a decent kid, but you have to work the four hours in order to get a break," the manager says.*

"I can only take a break after I work? What if that doesn't make sense umbrella-wise?" Benji asks.

"That's what I said, kid. You work your four hours, you get your break."

Benji goes back to his station, confused. He understands the rules to mean that for every shift of four hours or longer, he is entitled to a thirty-minute break, taken not necessarily on a whim, but not at the end of four hours either. If he can only take a thirty-minute break at the end of four hours, then a four-hour shift becomes a four-and-a-half-hour shift. This is confusing. Benji thinks break time should be based on conversation with his coworkers about the flow of traffic through the, er, umbrella factory. Plus, and he didn't mention this to the head guy because he's not a narc,† it was his coworker who told him to go on break, and he just listened because he's new.

"Dude?" Benji gets his coworker's attention. I'm not sure how noisy an umbrella belt line is — let's imagine a seventeen-year-old gesticulating wildly. "Just got in frickin' trouble for taking a break."

"Totally sucks," says coworker Dude.

More mumbling ensues, and because people under the age of eighteen always seem to understand each other, even when both are using earbuds, Benji emerges with the impression that

---

*   He really, really does look like a decent kid, and I'm not just saying that because I'm his mom.
†   This is a line from a Sandra Bullock movie that I can't think of right now. Her accent is super strong in the scene, and she's trying to say, "I'm not a narc," but it comes out, "I'm not a nahc."

the information provided by the senior manager is incorrect and that Dude at the next umbrella stand, who incidentally has the sickest sneakers, knows what time it is. Which does not literally mean he knows what time it is; it means he knows what's up, as in when breaks are allowed and not allowed. According to the coworker, the break is allowed at any point during your four-hour shift, as long as you intend to work at least four hours, and you have the approval of your manager.

Now the question is: Does the manager have the right to withhold the break until four hours have passed, as he says he will, and turn a four-hour shift into a four-and-a-half-hour shift? Or does he have to allow the workers to take their break at any point of their choosing during the four-hour shift? Or do the breaks have to be mutually agreed upon and scheduled in advance?

This is probably why a lot of people end up in law school. They are working in umbrella factories, trying to answer complex questions with very little information, and then they say to themselves, *We need a lawyer to figure this out. Might as well become one.*

Benji races home and tells me this whole story and asks me what he should do. Just kidding. He's a seventeen-year-old boy. He does not race anywhere; he ambles. Plus, he doesn't normally ask me for advice. Here's how I find out: A few weeks after the incident with his boss, my sister and Benji and I are at a sports bar for dinner, and the food is taking unusually long to arrive. My sister asks Benji how his new job is going, and that's when he tells us what's been happening.

My sister is a lawyer and therefore has already been to law school. She understands the ins and outs of umbrella factory shift work and break legislation.

"I don't know the answer," she says. *Oh*. I guess either law school was a long time ago or she missed the one lecture that is actually relevant.

"But I do know this," she continues. "All the rules about working, and breaks, and factories are set by different regulatory bodies, not only by your boss. There are real rules about how long people can work and how long their breaks can be."

"Who sets these?" Benji asks.

My sister explains to Benji where to look for these rules. In the province of Quebec, there is a government office that takes care of workers' rights and has a detailed website, email addresses, and phone numbers to call to get answers to your questions.

Before Benji can ask for what he wants, he needs to inform himself of the rules. He needs to call the government office that sets the policies for factory workers and find out exactly what he's entitled to. Then, armed with the correct information, he can speak to his boss about the break.

So many times we get caught up in our own stories. For example:

- We might think that Benji is an employee, and he should respect whatever his boss says.
- We might think that four hours in a row is too much for poor Benji, and he should be able to take his break whenever he wants in the four hours or four and a half hours, or three and a half hours, depending on our interpretation of the rules.
- We might want to conduct a workflow analysis of umbrella factory work and base the break timing on the results of our Pareto chart, or process flow, or something else operational.

The truth is, most of the time, there is an actual right and true answer. We don't need to depend on our own theories and speculation. Our job, or the worker's — in this case, Benji — is to find out what the rules are and then follow them.

Alternate Universe Analysis

Imagine Benji contacts the government agency, and they tell him that the rule is he can only take a break after working four hours, regardless of the workload. Benji can go back to the boss and tell him he was right, but he doesn't have to. He can just continue to work his shifts, taking a break after four hours, and knowing that he has no right to argue with the policy.

Imagine Benji contacts the government agency, and they tell him that when working a four-hour shift, he is entitled to one fifteen-minute break taken after two hours. Benji now has a choice. He can get this information in writing, and go back to his boss, and show it to him. He can then suggest that the law be followed, and that the break times be adjusted accordingly. Or he can mentally file it under "Things I know about my workplace," and decide not to argue right now. He takes breaks when the boss wants him to, knowing that he has leverage should he need to use it.

I can also imagine a situation where my son is so discouraged by the lack of adherence to policy that he decides he no longer wants to work in an umbrella factory.

He examines his options and perhaps determines that he is better suited to something else — like, say, a frozen yogurt shop.

Conclusion

I'm about twelve years old, and my family goes to Florida for winter break. We are staying in two apartments with my aunts, uncles, cousins, and cousins' girlfriends and boyfriends (all of whom are at least ten years older than my sister and me). Airbnb and couch surfing have not been invented yet, so staying in apartments feels like a low-rent option. You have to make your own bed, and there is no free breakfast. But the complex has a pool or two, and it has easy access to the beach. There is a game room with tabletop *Space Invaders*.

Lessons learned on this trip include, but are not limited to, the following:

- *Quincy* is a great TV show. Police procedurals, or mysteries that are cleared up in a one-hour episode, are fun to watch, and you get the hang of guessing that it's not the guy you think it is but someone who appeared for three seconds in Minute Twelve of the show.

- If you rent an apartment on vacation, you have more room to spread out. Yes, you might have to do the same chores you have at home, but you gain a living room, a kitchen, and, in this case, a balcony with a view.

- It is possible to make sure your kids are close with their cousins even if they are very far apart in age and live in different cities, but you have to invest the time and effort to make it work. By spending vacations together, we built connections and memories and inside jokes that we still laugh over today.

- Literary themes are more complicated than English teachers would have you believe. My homework that week was to read *Animal Farm* by George Orwell, which looked innocent with those cartoon pigs on the cover but turned out to be fraught with Communist discourse and other things that were way over my head. I remember walking around the apartment, wringing my hands, and wailing, "But I don't know what the *theme* is!" I believed I would get a zero on the book report, which would cause me to fail English, which would mean that *all* my grades would drop by association, and I would therefore never get into college.

Nothing much has changed. I still love Jack Klugman,* still have mixed feelings about hotel stays vs. vacation apartment rentals, and am still a little insecure about my ability to determine a literary theme. However, since I'm the one who wrote

---

* Jack Klugman played the medical examiner on the show *Quincy*. He died in 2012 at the age of ninety.

this book, I know for sure what the themes are, and I'm going to review them here, for myself, as a double check.

The first theme of the book is that speaking up for yourself works. Many people are afraid to ask for what they want because they don't know how. You have a better chance of getting what you want if you ask for it than if you don't, even if your technique is not perfect, even if you stumble. In contrast, if you do nothing, it is 100 percent certain that your situation will not change. If you speak up and try your best, chances are you will be able to get at least some of what you want.

The second theme is that if at first you don't succeed, you have to be prepared to keep trying. For example, if email doesn't work, try the phone. If a phone call doesn't work, go in person, and be your charming self. Same is true of people. As in the airplane-seat story, if you try the person in front of you, and they don't want to unrecline their airplane seat, ask the flight attendant for help. If the flight attendant can't help you, contact the airline when you land. When asking for what you want, it's useful to map out an escalation procedure — Plans A, B, and C — that you may or may not need to use, depending on the situation.

When it comes to interpersonal issues, and we want someone else to change, we have to think about Theme Three: It's okay to put yourself and your needs ahead of someone else's. If one of you (such as the host) wants to start dinner at 5 p.m., and one of you (such as the guest) is always late, you aren't both going to get your way. Therefore, it's acceptable for you to put your needs first, ahead of the other person's need to be late, as we learned in the meatballs story. If you choose to ignore the problem instead of establishing clear guidelines for your family event, know that you are making a conscious decision to choose the other person's needs ahead of your own. If you continue to do this, you will not be able to get what you want or need. I suggest that you spend some time working on this issue, either personally or with a professional, and then come back and pick up the book again. I think we can work together.

Theme Four is about compromise and creativity. If you can't get exactly what you want, what else can you get? When someone denies your request, I want you to immediately start brainstorming alternatives and determining what you are prepared to live with. Think about the kid on the playground, the onesie in the baby store, and the cellphone at dinner. Each of those stories showed that part of asking for what you need is figuring out exactly what you are willing to live with. I expect you to understand what your limits are and ask for a compromise. Don't waste time getting stuck on what "might have been." Go immediately to what is and what you can make happen.

The fifth theme is about people and communication and relationships. I've introduced you to my husband, Dave; and my three kids, Ezra/B (age nineteen), Benji/Beno (seventeen), and Liberty (thirteen). You've met my sister, who is usually media-shy; my great-uncle, who passed away while this book was being written; my great-aunt; and my dad. You've met many of my friends, past coworkers, knitting buddies, and book club members. All these relationships weave you into the fabric of my life and let you see that communication needs to be ongoing and clear to be effective. (This may not be a theme. I told you I struggled a bit with literary analysis.)

The sixth theme is about the responsibility to complain effectively. We ask for what we want so that we can get our french fries, our dresses returned, our problems solved. Yes, in many cases we stand to gain personally. Even an employee with fresher breath stands to benefit my pocketbook in the long run. But part of the reason we are speaking up is to make the world a better place for the next person. Even when it's too late to fix the problem for ourselves, we still believe fundamentally that it needs to be fixed for the next person in line. That's why I get up in the morning and resolve complaints all day, that's why I travel from coast to coast teaching people how to ask for what they want and need, and that's also why I wrote this book.

I'm so glad you chose to read it.

Thank you.

Acknowledgments

Thank you, Jules, for quietly ordering fries that never came. Thirty-seven years have passed since that pivotal moment, and so much of my work and who I am comes from those non-arriving fries. Also thank you to Tals for being a part of the fries and everything before and after.

Thank you to Taali for telling me that I should write a blog, and Steph for saying, "I'm sure you'll find something to say."

Molls, I remember walking down the street with you and saying, "I may actually sell this book." Thank you for celebrating prematurely with me.

Thank you to my knitting friends, my book club, and my elaborate and dedicated support system. I love having you all on speed dial/speed text and don't know where I would be without you. Well, I know for sure I would be alone in a ditch, but I don't know which one.

Thank you to Uncle Avi z'l* (whom I miss desperately) and Auntie Dora, who believed in me and supported me, no questions asked. Okay, maybe a few questions asked, but always there for me. Thank you, Lulu, for being involved in this book every step of the way and being a great sounding board no matter what was going on with you. GTY. Love.

To all my aunts, uncles, cousins, nieces, nephews: You are the best cheerleaders anyone could ask for, and I love and thank you individually and collectively.

Now let's talk writing gratitude:

I am indebted to Donna Talarico-Beerman for having the vision to start HippoCamp, which has changed my life and the lives of so many writers.

If it weren't for HippoCamp, I would never have met Veronica Park, my trusted agent and good friend. Veronica, thank you for sticking with me, believing in me, and knowing I could do it. BDE, etc.

Thank you, Georgia, Munro, Kim, Tristy, Kristen, Sandra, Ami, Tona, and the rest of the New World Library team, for making this manuscript better than I ever thought possible. Thank you, Dana and everyone at Kaye Publicity, for helping me spread the gospel of complaining.

Immediate family:

To my dad: I finally surprised you, I think. Thank you for all your support, moral and otherwise.

To my sister: Thank you for making Friday night dinner every week until the book was finished. Your generosity knows

---

* Z'l is short for *zichrono l'vracha*, which means "of blessed memory." It's a Jewish version of "May he rest in peace."

no bounds. I love you so much and appreciate you, Paul, Sarah, and Jack every single day.

To Davidle: Thank you for asking me to marry you on our first date. Happy to have checked you off my list as early as possible. I love you so much.

To Beanie, Beno, and Lib-Lib: I love you all to pieces. Thank you for making me laugh so hard that I look like a dying eel.

And to everyone on my team and yours: Here's to another million years together and lots more books. May you always get the fries you've ordered.

Endnotes

p. 3   *We base our decision on whether we think we'll be successful*:
       John W. Huppertz and Eric Mower, "An Effort Model of First-
       Stage Complaining Behavior," *Journal of Consumer Satisfaction,
       Dissatisfaction and Complaining Behavior* 27 (2014): 6–18.

p. 9   *"Standing up for yourself doesn't mean being a rude tyrant"*:
       Carolyn Steber, "11 Little Ways to Stand Up for Yourself Every
       Day, No Matter What," *Bustle*, June 30, 2016, https://www.bustle
       .com/articles/169607-11-little-ways-to-stand-up-for-yourself
       -every-day-no-matter-what.

p. 34 *the greater the service quality of the customer service representa-
       tive*: Aihie Osarenkhoe, Mabel Birungi Komunda, and Jotham
       Mbiito Byarugaba, "Service Quality as a Mediator of Customer
       Complaint Behaviour and Customer Loyalty," *International
       Review of Management and Marketing* 7 (2017): 197–208.

p. 55 *"The evidence that is available has clearly identified"*: Matylda
       Howard, Mary Louise Fleming, and Elizabeth Parker, "Pa-
       tients Do Not Always Complain When They Are Dissatisfied:

Implications for Service Quality and Patient Safety," *Journal of Patient Safety* 9, no. 4 (December 2013): 224–31.

p. 102　*Studies have shown that emotions like anxiety*: Laura D. Kubzansky and Ichiro Kawachi, "Review: Going to the Heart of the Matter: Do Negative Emotions Cause Coronary Heart Disease?," *Journal of Psychosomatic Research* 48 (2000): 323–37.

p. 129　*"When people show you who they are"*: Joan Podrazik, "Oprah's Life Lesson from Maya Angelou: When People Show You Who They Are, Believe Them," *Huffington Post*, video, April 14, 2013.

p. 165　*"Whenever possible, talk to an actual person"*: David Hochman, "How to Complain," *AARP Bulletin*, September 2016, 32.

p. 173　*"avoid complaining on social media"*: Christopher Mele, "How to Complain and Get Results," *New York Times*, June 15, 2017, https://www.nytimes.com/2017/06/15/smarter-living/consumer-complaint-writing-letter.html.

p. 174　*"they won't ever call customer service"*: Rosemary Counter, "Make. It. Right." *MoneySense*, June 2016, 13–15.

About the Author

Amy Fish serves as ombudsman (otherwise known as Chief Complaints Officer) at Concordia University in Montreal, where she responds to complaints from students, faculty, staff, and the community and resolves disputes. She has written for *Huffington Post Canada*, *Reader's Digest*, *Hippocampus Magazine*, the *Globe and Mail*, and professional journals such as *Long Term Care Today*. She is called upon as a complaint expert by CBC Marketplace and CTV nightly news, and her work has appeared on the websites *Finding Your Bliss*, *Wise-Women Canada*, and *Montreal Mom*. Amy blogs regularly at www.complaintdepartmentblog.blogspot.com. She teaches workshops such as "The Art of Complaining Effectively," "ABCDE of Resolving Complaints," "Kvetching 101," and "How to Be Funny in Nonfiction," including at the prestigious Hippo-Camp 18 in Pennsylvania. Amy has spoken at various conferences around the world. She lives with her family in Montreal.

www.amyfishwrites.com